TOP **10**
NEW ENGLAND

CONTENTS

NEW ENGLAND

INTRODUCING

Fall foliage in Vermont

WELCOME TO
NEW ENGLAND

With stunning natural landscapes, rich and varied histories, and buzzing cultural scenes, the six states that make up New England have it all. Don't want to miss a thing? With Top 10 New England, you'll enjoy the very best the region has to offer.

Nowhere does fall scenery quite like New England. This bucolic region is famed for its autumn display, with leaf-peeping opportunities abounding in all six states – whether you're hiking through crimson woods in the mountains of Vermont or driving through picture-perfect villages in New Hampshire. But New England is beautiful beyond the fall. Spring and summer see vacationers flock to Cape Cod and its nearby islands (enchanting Martha's Vineyard and Nantucket), where breezy beaches and charming towns await. Winter, meanwhile, promises snowy hikes,

Quaint Newport, Rhode Island

toboggan rides, and epic skiing in places like the Litchfield Hills (Connecticut) and Sugarloaf (Maine).

There's plenty of history here, too. New England's Indigenous story dates back thousands of years, while its settler history is one of the richest in the US (both can be explored in Maine's Plimoth Patuxet museum). This region is also famed for its gorgeous Gilded Age mansions (in Newport), fascinating industrial history (in Lowell), and trailblazing universities (Harvard and Yale). But when it comes to New England's history, one event always dominates the conversation: the American Revolution. It all began in the towns of Concord and Lexington, but you'll find the best concentration of sights along Boston's famed Freedom Trail.

Talking of Boston, the region's capital is a great place to start your adventure. As well as being packed with historic sites, it's also the area's main cultural hub, home to top art galleries, acclaimed restaurants, lively LGBTQ+ venues, animated sports venues, and so much more.

So, where to start? With Top 10 New England, of course. This pocket-sized guide gets to the heart of the region with simple lists of 10, expert local knowledge and comprehensive maps, helping you turn an ordinary trip into an extraordinary one.

THE STORY OF
NEW ENGLAND

Since the early days of their history, New England's six states have been epicenters of revolutions, industrial innovation, and equal rights movements – and continue to be so today. Here's the story of how the region came to be.

Indigenous Beginnings

Well over ten thousand years before the region's European colonists arrived, New England was home to a number of Indigenous communities. Over the ages, distinct groups emerged in the region, including the Narragansett of modern-day Rhode Island, the Wabanaki of present-day Maine, and the Wampanoag, a people whose territory includes Southeastern Massachusetts and its nearby islands. These Indigenous peoples lived in complex societies that fished, traded, and farmed across the region. Their rich agricultural knowledge – such as the use of fish as crop fertilizer and the practice of planting corn, beans, and squash together to maximize yield – would prove vital to the survival of European settlers.

Rising Tensions

Indigenous life changed for the worse in 1620 when a ship known as the *Mayflower* docked on the shores of modern-day Massachusetts. On board were the Pilgrims, a group of 102 travelers who had grown discontent with the Church of England and sought to practice their religion far from English rule. They built permanent settlements in New England (named by John Smith), and were followed across the ocean by waves of like-minded Puritans, who established the Massachusetts Bay Colony in 1630. With so many new arrivals, land and resources became increasingly scarce and tensions between the settlers and Indigenous peoples continued to rise. This reached a peak in the latter half of the 17th century, when the region was plunged

Depiction of Indigenous peoples in Maine

The Battle of Concord, during the American Revolution

into King Philip's War, a bloody conflict that eventually ended in victory for the colonists and the mass execution and banishment of local Indigenous peoples.

Revolution Ignites

Though the largely English colonists laid claim to the land for Britain, the vast distance between the two continents gave New Englanders little say in legislative decision-making for their new land. And while many had found prosperity in the region's whaling industry, the imposition of heavy taxes on imports across the colonies led to further economic frustration. New Englanders began talking rebellion and forming militias, and tensions reached a boiling point in 1773. Enraged by a British law known as the Tea Act (which was perceived as another attempt at taxation without representation), a small faction of Bostonians boarded an English ship and tossed its tea shipment into the sea. In response, the British shut the harbor and declared martial law.

Rebellion eventually ignited into revolution in 1775, when New England colonists and British soldiers clashed in the Battles of Lexington and Concord – the first skirmishes of the Revolutionary War. A year later, the Declaration of Independence was adopted by the colonists and led to the foundation of a new country (the United States). New Englanders were now Americans and after nearly a decade fighting, they defeated the British army in 1783.

Moments in History

1620
The Pilgrims land on the Massachusetts coast and establish Plymouth, one of the oldest surviving English settlements in North America.

1675
King Philip's War – a conflict between English colonies and Indigenous populations – causes widespread devastation across New England, leading to the displacement of many Indigenous communities.

1773
Hundreds of chests of tea are dumped into Boston Harbor to protest the Tea Act, leading to outrage in London and sparking the Revolutionary War.

1775
The opening gunshot is fired during the Battles of Lexington and Concord, plunging the colonies into war with Britain. The conflict lasts until 1783, with the colonists claiming victory under the command of George Washington.

1836
Ralph Waldo Emerson publishes "Nature", a celebrated essay that sets the foundation for the 19th-century transcendentalism movement.

1850
The first National Women's Rights Convention takes place in Worcester, Massachusetts, with hundreds of participants demanding equality and suffrage.

1912
The Bread and Roses Strike, a lengthy protest against pay cuts held largely by women and immigrants, takes place in Lawrence, Massachusetts.

1965
Dr. Martin Luther King Jr. leads a major civil rights rally on Boston Common, drawing over 20,000 spectators.

2004
Massachusetts becomes the first US state to legalize same-sex marriage, setting the standard for nationwide equality.

Economic Boom and Social Reform

Buoyant from the Revolution, the US was spurred into another: the American Industrial Revolution. New England was at the center of this booming trade, with its rushing rivers transforming the region into an industrialization hub in the 19th century – the Massachusetts town of Lowell is often regarded as one of the foundational sites of the Industrial Revolution thanks to its hydro-powered mills and factories. This spike in manufacturing led to a steep increase in immigration, drawing people from Ireland, Italy, and a wealth of other nations to big cities like Boston and Providence, and sowing the seeds of the region's rich cultural identity that still thrives today.

Amid the economic boom, reform movements also took root across the region. Women's rights became a popular topic of conversation and led to large-scale conferences like the National Women's Rights Convention. The onset of the Civil War also thrust abolitionism into the spotlight, with each of the six free states of New England serving as safe havens for enslaved people

Acclaimed American poet Emily Dickinson

Harvard University, in Cambridge, Massachusetts

escaping persecution. Around this time, some of North America's literary greats were penning their most notable works across the region, with Henry David Thoreau – a leading figure in transcendentalism – and the prolific poet Emily Dickinson being just a few of the 19th-century authors who called New England home.

Economic Decline and Social Unrest

The region's fortunes began to decline in the 20th century. Between the two world wars, New England was marred by economic instability and rising unemployment, and while New Deal programs provided some relief, the region underwent a gradual decline. The once-thriving manufacturing industry was particularly hard-hit, with textile production largely moving overseas.

In spite of this downfall, the region continued to be a beacon for rights movements, with Boston's Roxbury neighborhood serving as a cradle for the regional civil rights movement throughout the 1960s. New England's universities were also gaining prestige around this time, laying the groundwork for future prominence in the fields of science and technology. Tech-focused institutions such as MIT and Harvard would later put the area front-and-center of America's digital era.

New England Today

New England witnessed a tourism boom in the late 20th and early 21st centuries, with wealthy Bostonians and New Yorkers buying vacation homes in areas like the Berkshires and Cape Cod, while others began flocking to the region to see its fall foliage. This influx has brought economic profit. However, overtourism has also become an issue in the region, and many rural towns are still grappling with solutions.

By the 21st century, New England had cemented itself as a region defined by its world-class colleges and economic innovation. Prestigious universities like Harvard, MIT, and Yale remain pillars of global excellence, while tech-focused startups have excelled in the Boston and Cambridge area, fostering further economic growth. The region remains a champion of social progression, too. In 2004, the Massachusetts Supreme Court in Boston legalized same-sex marriage – the first US state to do so – while 2021 saw the election of Michelle Wu as city mayor, the first woman and person of color to be elected to the office.

TOP 10
EXPERIENCES

Planning the perfect trip to New England? Whether you're visiting for the first time or making a return trip, there are some things you simply shouldn't miss out on. To make the most of your time – and to enjoy the very best this storied region has to offer – be sure to add these experiences to your list.

1 Try a lobster boil

Lobsters are abundant in the cold waters off New England, and making a lobster boil is one of the region's most time-honored culinary traditions. Cape Cod (p26) is a go-to for the dish, but when it comes to undisputed master of lobster, there's no beating Maine's famous Lobster Festival (p81).

2 Go leaf-peeping

Think of New England and you'll probably picture the region in all its fall glory. Each of the six states promises gorgeous leafy scenery, but Vermont is a particular highlight thanks to its Green Mountain Byway, a scenic road that weaves through quaint villages and forests.

3 Marvel at gentle giants

New England offers some of the finest whale-watching opportunities in the Lower 48, with humpback, minke, and finback whales all frequenting its shores. Numerous tour boats operate across Massachusetts and Maine: Bar Harbor (p30) and Provincetown (p27) are both popular setting-off points.

4 Discover Boston's revolutionary roots

No city has a revolutionary history quite like Boston. Packed with storied sites, this historic city is best explored via the Freedom Trail (p25), a route that leads visitors to key sites from the city's revolutionary past, including Boston Common and Granary Burying Ground.

5 Admire the architecture

From 1600s-era shacks to 19th-century cathedrals, New England is home to a wealth of architecture. To see early settler homes, head to Old Wethersfield *(p103)* in Connecticut. Prefer Gilded Age opulence? Rhode Island's Breakers *(p42)* is the go-to.

6 Hike the Appalachians

Lace up your hiking boots; it's time to hit the trails. The forests and peaks of the Appalachian mountains can be explored throughout New England, with particularly scenic pockets including the spectacular White Mountains *(p34)* and Green Mountains *(p40)*.

7 Take a literary pilgrimage

Jack Kerouac, Mark Twain, Edith Wharton: numerous writers have put pen to paper in New England. For an insight into their works, visit their homes-turned-museums *(p52)*, or take a trip to Walden Pond, renowned for its association with Henry David Thoreau.

8 Explore Indigenous culture

Long before Europeans settled here, New England was home to several Indigenous communities. Today, fascinating sites such as the Mashantucket Pequot Museum *(p107)* and Plimoth Patuxet *(p46)* offer insight into their customs and daily lives.

9 Escape to the seaside

Loved by the Kennedys and famed for its postcard-worthy resorts, Cape Cod *(p26)* and the beachy islands *(p58)* off the region's coastline (Martha's Vineyard, where *Jaws* was filmed, and Nantucket) are New England's favorite vacation spots.

10 Cruise along Lake Champlain

Sometimes known as the "Sixth Great Lake," Lake Champlain *(p62)* is a prime destination for watersports in interior New England. Canoeing and kayaking opportunities abound here, while sunset cruises are popular, too.

ITINERARIES

Marveling at fall foliage, dining on lobster, visiting centuries-old landmarks: there's a lot to see and do in New England. With places to eat, drink or take in the view, these itineraries offer ways to spend 2 days in Boston and 7 days in the region.

2 DAYS IN BOSTON

Day 1

Morning
Start the day with a trip to Acorn Street, a treasured Beacon Hill *(p23)* photo spot that's dotted with rustic cobblestones and picturesque row houses. Next, make your way to two idyllic green spaces – Boston Common and Public Garden *(p22)*. First, stroll through the Public Garden, marveling at polished statues and watching the Swan Boats along the way, before entering neighboring Boston Common. Established in 1634, this site is the oldest city park in the nation, with towering monuments, curious squirrels darting about, and the Frog Pond (an ice rink in winter). By now you've probably worked up an appetite. Head to nearby JM Curley *(jmcurleyboston.com)*, where tasty burgers are up for grabs.

> 🍴 **EAT**
> If you're in need of a quick bite as you explore the North End, pop in to Bova's Bakery *(bovabakery boston.net)*. This spot has been a local favorite since 1932 thanks to its cannoli, specialty cookies, bread, cakes, and other Italian favorites.

Afternoon
After a hearty lunch, it's time to hit the Freedom Trail *(p25)*. Begin at the Granary Burying Ground *(p22)* to pay your respects to iconic American luminaries, then continue northeast to visit sites like King's Chapel and the Massachusetts State House *(p22)* before arriving at Faneuil Hall *(p22)*, formerly a popular place for impassioned political speeches. Pop into neighboring Quincy Market, which is filled with food stalls and shops. Once you've snagged the perfect souvenir, head up Mercantile Street to North End to visit Paul Revere House *(p22)* and Copps Hill Burying Ground. End the day with a feast at Regina Pizzeria *(pizzeria regina.com)*, a cozy spot with top pies.

Day 2

Morning
Today kicks off with a stroll through Chinatown, a bustling district anchored by a traditional Chinese gateway. Fuel up on caffeine with a Vietnamese iced coffee at Pho Pasteur *(phopasteur*

Boston Common during the fall season

boston.net), then head for some retail therapy at Essex Corner *(50 Essex St)* to peruse trinkets. To continue your shopping spree, walk along Boylston Street to reach the Back Bay neighborhood. Here, you'll encounter boutique stores along Newbury Street, but be sure to also make a quick pit stop to admire the ornate Trinity Church. Once you're ready for lunch, seek out the Banks Fish House *(thebanksboston.com)* for a lobster roll and a bowl of clam chowder.

Afternoon

Make your way to Back Bay Station and hop on the "T" to Andrew Station to explore South Boston, where two sites in particular are worth visiting. The first is Carson Beach, a great spot for swimming and beach volleyball; the second is Dorchester Heights, where you'll discover the crucial role that this area played during the Revolutionary War. After all this activity, reward yourself with a trip to the iconic L Street Tavern *(p76)* before hopping back on the "T" to return to the heart of Boston, for a lavish dinner at Oya *(p89)*.

Pretty Newbury Street, known for its boutiques

> 📷 **VIEW**
> Searching for a truly remarkable perspective on the city? Head up to Back Bay's View Boston *(viewboston.com)* to find 360-degree views from the 52nd floor of Prudential Tower.

Freedom Trail
Copps Hill Burying Ground
NORTH END
Regina Pizzeria
Paul Revere House
WATERFRONT
Charles River
WEST END
BEACON HILL
Quincy Market
Faneuil Hall
Acorn Street
Massachusetts State House
King's Chapel
①
Granary Burying Ground
DOWNTOWN
Public Garden
Boston Common
JM Curley
Essex Corner
0 meters 500
0 yards 500
ACK BAY
Pho Pasteur
②
Oya
Chinatown Gate
inity urch
Banks Fish House
Back Bay Station
SUBWAY

South Boston
from Back Bay Station 1.5 miles (2 km)
SOUTH BOSTON
Dorchester Heights
DAY 2 SUBWAY
to Andrew Station 1.5 miles (2 km)
Andrew Station
L Street Tavern
Carson Beach
0 meters 1000
0 yards 1000

7 DAYS IN NEW ENGLAND

Day 1

There's no more scenic place to start your adventure than Cape Cod. About a two-hour drive from Boston, this pretty peninsula is Massachusetts' favorite vacation spot. It's skirted by sandy beaches – including Mayflower Beach, a great place for some sunbathing – and dotted with fun-loving resorts like Provincetown (p27), your base for the night. Located at the very tip of Cape Cod, P-Town (as the locals call it) is a liberal and lively place, with quirky shops and buzzy bars (head to Commercial Street for the best ones).

Day 2

Leisurely vacationers could happily linger in Cape Cod for the week, but there's so much more to see. After a night in P-Town, swing down south – stopping at Marconi Beach for a

Colorful cottages on Martha's Vineyard

morning walk – and make your way to Hyannis (p27). From here, you can hop on the car ferry to Nantucket (the ride's just over an hour). Once you've settled into your accommodation, rent a bike and start exploring the island. You could brush up on the area's maritime history at the Nantucket Whaling Museum (p54), feast on fresh oysters at Cru (crunantucket.com), or spend the day by the beach (Surfside is a go-to).

Day 3

Nantucket's quite small, so rather than spending another day here, take the passenger ferry to Martha's Vineyard (p85) – opt for a high-speed ferry and you'll be there in an hour. Alight at Oak Bluffs, a settlement beloved for its historic cottages, and admire the

> **TRANSPORTATION**
> Taking a car on the Nantucket and Martha's Vineyard ferries requires prior planning. Be sure to book your tickets weeks, or even months in advance if you're planning to visit during peak summer season.

gorgeous architecture. Come afternoon, hop on a rental bike and cycle over to bustling Edgartown, where tasty seafood awaits at Seafood Shanty *(31 Dock St)*. Post-meal, head back to the ferry for another night on Nantucket.

Day 4

It's time to say goodbye to the islands today, and to Massachusetts. Take the boat back to the mainland and head west into Rhode Island. Though tiny, the state offers grandiose opulence in the form of Newport *(p42)*, a coastal city brimming with Gilded Age mansions like The Breakers *(p42)*. Take a tour of the building, then stroll along the Cliff Walk, a windy path that hugs the shoreline. As the sun sets, feast on Italian food at Giusto *(p101)* before bedding down for the night in Newport.

Day 5

A 40-minute drive from Newport takes you to Providence *(p95)*, the state capital. Drop by the RISD Museum *(p51)* for a morning filled with fine arts, then explore the city's thriving Portuguese dining scene – Aguardente *(aguardente. com)* offers top-tier Iberian classics. After lunch, head back to Newport

for an afternoon of shopping along Bowen's Wharf and an early night.

Day 6

You're off to Connecticut today. From Newport, drive towards Litchfield, pausing in Hartford to pop into the Mark Twain House *(p52)* and fuel up on Italian cuisine at Treva *(trevact.com)*. Then, continue on to Litchfield. Cocooned in the countryside, this wonderful town promises picture-perfect houses, independent shops, and gorgeous natural scenery. Take a walk through the White Memorial Conservation Center *(whitememorialcc.org)*, before heading back to the center for a local dinner.

Day 7

Spend your final day in nature. You could hike through leafy Mount Tom State Park *(p39)* – take the Tower Trail for especially scenic views – or spend the day relaxing at Lake Waramaug *(p38)*. You're not far from Boston now, but be sure to stop by Woodbury on your way back; the antique shops *(p74)* here promise lovely souvenirs.

Admiring the fall scenery at Lake Waramaug, Connecticut

TOP 10 HIGHLIGHTS

Fall in the Green Mountains, Vermont

EXPLORE THE
HIGHLIGHTS

There are some sights in New England
you simply shouldn't miss, and it's these
attractions that make the Top 10.
Discover what makes each one a
must-see on the following pages.

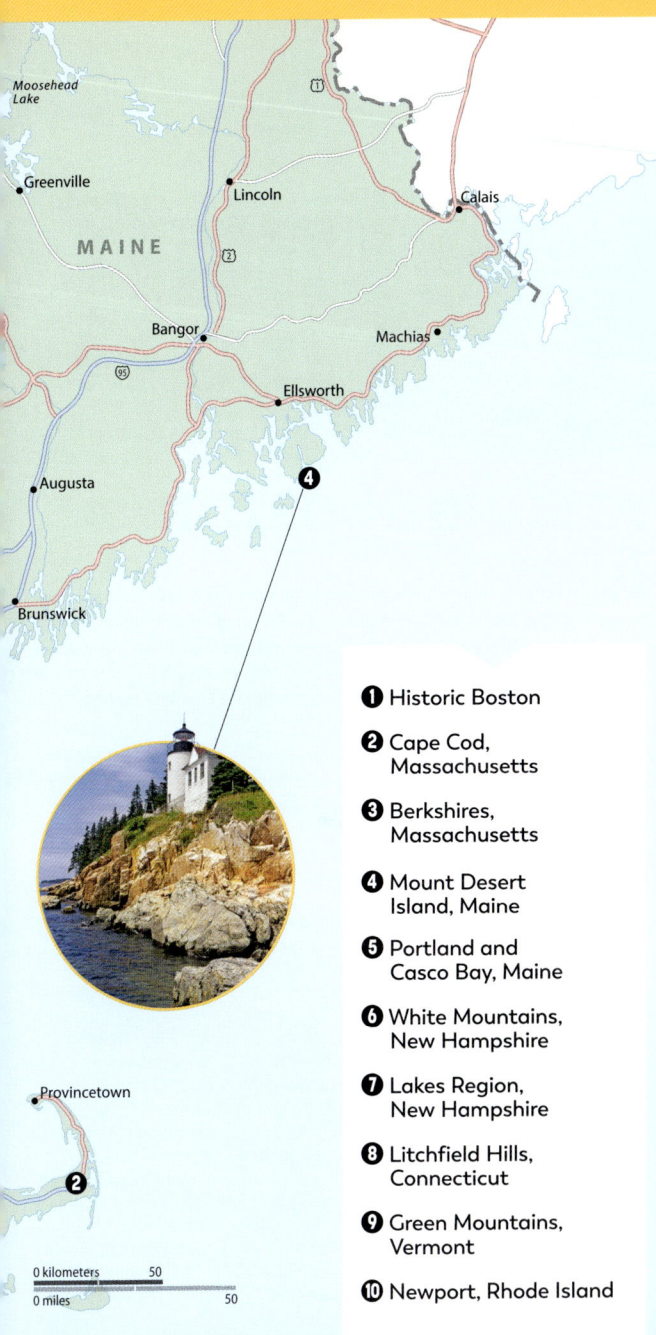

Moosehead Lake

Greenville

Lincoln

Calais

MAINE

2

Bangor

Machias

95

Ellsworth

Augusta

4

Brunswick

Provincetown

2

0 kilometers   50
0 miles   50

❶ Historic Boston

❷ Cape Cod, Massachusetts

❸ Berkshires, Massachusetts

❹ Mount Desert Island, Maine

❺ Portland and Casco Bay, Maine

❻ White Mountains, New Hampshire

❼ Lakes Region, New Hampshire

❽ Litchfield Hills, Connecticut

❾ Green Mountains, Vermont

❿ Newport, Rhode Island

HISTORIC BOSTON

⚐ S1–X6

Founded in 1630 by Puritans who envisioned their colony as a shining beacon to the world, Boston was among America's great urban centers – its patriots led the rebellion that grew into the American Revolution. Today, Boston remains at the forefront in politics, arts, and science, with colonial and Revolutionary landmarks alongside modern architecture.

1 Massachusetts State House

⚐ W3 ⌂ 24 Beacon St
⏱ 9am–5pm Mon–Fri

Completed in 1798, this legislative temple, with its ornate marble and paneled halls, was architect Charles Bulfinch's masterpiece, and the model for other state capitols around the country.

2 Boston Common

⚐ V4

Established in 1634, Boston's historic Common is a green space where concerts and plays are regularly held. Adjacent is the Public Garden, which offers Swan Boat rides on its tranquil pond.

3 Granary Burying Ground

⚐ W3

Featuring over 2,300 tombstones, this graveyard is the final resting place of some of Boston's famed personalities.

4 Faneuil Hall

⚐ X3 ⌂ Doch Sq

One of Boston's many Revolutionary sites, Faneuil Hall is where Samuel Adams issued a clarion call for revolt. The hall was partly funded by the slave trade, and debate ensues over renaming it.

5 Paul Revere House

⚐ X3 ⌂ 19 North Sq
⏱ 10am–5:15pm daily
ⓦ paulreverehouse.org

Revere's house, built around 1680, is the oldest in Boston. During a visit here you get an intimate look at the life of this key figure in the American Revolution.

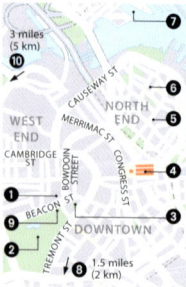

Neo-Classical Massachusetts State House

6 Old North Church

W X2 📍 193 Salem St
🕐 10am–5pm daily (from 11:30am Sun)
🌐 oldnorth.com

The Old North Church features minimal decor typical of a colonial house of worship. It is famous for the lanterns hung in its belfry, which were used to signal British troop movements.

7 USS Constitution

W1 📍 Charlestown Navy Yard, 1 Constitution Rd, Charlestown
🕐 9:30am–5pm daily
🌐 ussconstitution.org

The USS *Constitution*, a three-masted frigate, is the world's oldest commissioned warship. Called "Old Ironsides," this vessel has served in the US Navy since 1797. Its rich history is covered at the ship's museum.

8 Fenway Park

S5 📍 4 Jersey St
🕐 Hours vary, check website 🌐 mlb.com/redsox

Opened in 1912, Fenway Park is the oldest Major League Baseball (MLB) park. It's the home ground of the famed Boston Red Sox, the city's only MLB team.

9 Black Heritage Trail

V3 📍 46 Joy St
🌐 nps.gov/boaf

This trail in the city's Beacon Hill neighborhood links sights that played a key role in the struggle against segregation and slavery.

10 Harvard Yard

S1

America's first university, Harvard was founded in 1636 in Cambridge, a suburb of Boston. The grassy Harvard Yard (enclosed by 27 gates) is the oldest part of the campus. Free student-led tours offer a glimpse into life here.

Clockwise from right **Sign at the entrance to historic Fenway Park; interior of the Old North Church; enjoying a Swan Boat ride in the Public Garden, Boston Common**

A painting depicting the Battle of Lexington

Moments in Revolutionary History

1. Resistance to the Stamp Act (1765)
The king imposed a stamp duty on all published materials in the colonies, including newspapers. Angry Bostonians boycotted British goods in response.

2. Boston Massacre (1770)
On March 5, in front of the Massachusetts State House (p22), an angry mob of colonists taunted British guardsmen with insults, rocks, and snowballs. The soldiers opened fire, killing five. The first man killed was Crispus Attucks, a formerly enslaved man of African and Indigenous descent, who became an important symbol in the Civil Rights movement.

3. Samuel Adams' Tea Tax Speech (1773)
Adams' incendiary speech during a forum at the Old South Meeting House inspired the Boston Tea Party, the most subversive action undertaken yet in the debate over colonial secession.

4. Boston Tea Party (1773)
The city's most famous act of rebellion took place at Griffin's Wharf on December 16. Led by Samuel Adams, the Sons of Liberty boarded three British East India Company ships and dumped their cargo into the Boston Harbor, a watershed moment of colonial defiance.

5. Paul Revere's Ride (1775)
Revere rode to Lexington to warn revolutionaries Samuel Adams and John Hancock that British troops intended to arrest them. One of the bravest acts of the war, it would be immortalized in the Longfellow poem *Paul Revere's Ride*.

6. Battle of Lexington (1775)
Revere's ride was followed by the first exchange of fire between American militia, known as Minute Men, and British regulars on Lexington Green. Within weeks, the American Revolution had begun.

7. Battle of Bunker Hill (1775)
The colonists' fortification of Charlestown resulted in a fullscale British attack. Despite their defeat, the colonists' resolve was galvanized by this battle.

8. Washington Takes Command (1775)
George Washington, the Virginia plantation owner and former commander in chief of American forces during Queen Anne's War, assumed command of the Continental Army in Cambridge.

9. Fortification of Dorchester Heights (1776)
Fortifying the mouth of Boston Harbor with a captured cannon, Washington put the Royal Navy under his guns and forced a British retreat from the city.

10. Declaration of Independence (1776)
On July 4, the colonies rejected all allegiance to the British Crown. In Boston, independence was declared from the Royal Governor's headquarters, today known as the Massachusetts State House.

THE FREEDOM TRAIL

**Freedom Trail sign
for landmarks**

Boston has more sights directly related to the American Revolution than any other city in the US. The most important of these, as well as some that relate to other freedoms gained by Bostonians, form the city's Freedom Trail. Marked by a red line along the sidewalk (either paint or bricks), this historic trail snakes through Boston for 2.5 miles (4 km). It's easily walkable, beginning in the leafy Boston Common, the oldest public park in the US, and weaving through the historic center of the city. The trail then begins to stretch out as it meanders through the narrow streets of the North End to Charlestown, with a final climb up the Bunker Hill Monument, where the first major battle of the Revolutionary War, the Battle of Bunker Hill, was fought. Trail maps are available at the Boston Common Visitor Center, or at the Boston National Park headquarters at Faneuil Hall, where free, ranger-led walking tours are offered. For more information, see thefreedomtrail.org.

Bunker Hill Monument, commemorating the Revolutionary War

CAPE COD, MASSACHUSETTS

◪ G4–H4

Extending some 70 miles (113 km) into the sea, Cape Cod is shaped like an upraised arm, bent at the elbow, ending with the fist at Provincetown. Every summer, millions of visitors arrive to enjoy its boundless beaches, natural beauty, and pretty villages. It is also famous for its fishing fleets, which haul the sweetest scallops and richest tuna.

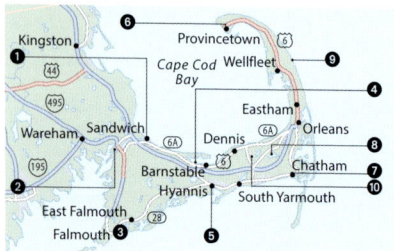

3 Falmouth
◪ N4

Perched on the tip of Cape Cod, Falmouth is a quintessential New England town with neat rows of houses and tall churches. Nearby, Woods Hole is home to several science institutions. The towns are connected by the picturesque Shining Sea bike path.

1 Sandwich Town Beach

A perfect spot for beachcombing, Town Beach offers gentle waves and warm waters, making it ideal for kids. It can be accessed from Cape Cod Canal or by a scenic boardwalk.

2 Cape Cod Canal

Built to save ships from the perilous Nantucket Shoals, this 7-mile- (12-km-) long canal marks the beginning of Cape Cod. Bike down its paths, or fish for bass and ferocious bluefish.

4 King's Highway

Also known as Route 6A, this historic US byway offers a scenic drive, connecting the

Strolling along Sandwich Town Beach

Colorful storefronts in Provincetown

charming villages of Cape Cod Bay, home to numerous artists' studios.

5 Hyannis
Thanks to its airport and two ferry lines to Nantucket and Martha's Vineyard, Hyannis is Cape Cod's market town and transportation hub.

> **TRANSPORTATION**
> Traveling around the Cape Cod peninsula with kids? Take Route 28, which features an array of fun pitstops, including mini-golf courses and popular ice-cream stands.

6 Provincetown
Popularly referred to as "P-Town," the Cape's most colorful community (p92) began as a Portuguese-American fishing village, before becoming a major art colony. It's now a leading LGBTQ+ destination.

7 Chatham
Home to an iconic lighthouse dating back to 1808, Chatham has ever-shifting barrier beaches, frequented by seabirds and seals.

8 Nickerson State Park
🏠 Rte 6A, Brewster
🌐 mass.gov/locations
This parkland is dotted with glacial kettle ponds. Visitors can canoe and fish here, watch rare songbirds, and camp at over 400 sites.

9 Cape Cod National Seashore Beaches
🏠 Rte 6, Eastham
🕐 9am–5pm daily
In 1961, this area of 43,607 acres (17,647 ha), stretching across several beaches, ponds and a sizable expanse of forested area, was designated as a "National Seashore."

> **PROVINCETOWN'S ARTIST COLONY**
>
> Artists, writers, and poets have long been inspired by P-Town's natural beauty. Its first art school opened in 1901. Since then, many prominent artists, including Jackson Pollock, Mark Rothko, and Edward Hopper, have spent time here. Over the years, the roster of famous resident writers has included Tennessee Williams and Eugene O'Neill.

10 Cape Cod Rail Trail
This invigorating 25-mile (40-km) rail trail begins in Dennis, meanders through fields and forest, skirts a pretty fishing harbor, and then follows dune cliffs to end at the town of Wellfleet. Along the way, soak up the views of the stunning Cape Cod National Seashore.

Biking along the Cape Cod Rail Trail

BERKSHIRES, MASSACHUSETTS

B2–B3 berkshires.org

The natural beauty of the Massachusetts Berkshires beckons visitors in every season – whether it's summertime picnics on the Tanglewood lawns, enjoying outdoor contemporary dance shows at Jacob's Pillow Dance Festival, strolling through the resplendent foliage of fall, or hiking mountaintop trails to soak up sweeping views.

1 Williamstown

This historic village at the edge of Mount Greylock attracts art lovers to The Clark (p49) and Williams College, known for their extensive art collections.

2 Mount Greylock

30 Rockwell Rd, Lanesborough; 413 499 4262

At 3,491 ft (1,064 m) high, Greylock is the highest point in Massachusetts. In the past, US authors Nathaniel Hawthorne and Henry David Thoreau climbed it. It is accessed by hiking trails or the seasonal road.

3 Hancock Shaker Village

Now a museum and a working farm, Hancock (p46) was one of the most influential communities of the celibate religious sect of Shakers. Its Round Stone Barn is an architectural masterpiece.

4 Tanglewood Music Center

The summer home of the Boston Symphony Orchestra since 1937, Tanglewood Music Center also hosts jazz, chamber music, popular music concerts, and a summer music education program.

5 Stockbridge

This slow-paced village was once home to renowned American illustrator Norman Rockwell (1894–1978) who drew inspiration

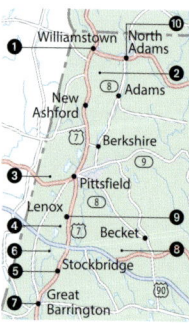

Lovely Main Street in Williamstown, Vermont

> 🍴 **EAT**
> Head to the deli behind Rubiner's Cheesemongers (*264 Main St, Great Barrington; 413 528 0488*) for gourmet sandwiches, with local cheeses.

from its people and buildings for his nostalgic portrayals of rural American life. The village is also known for the Red Lion Inn, one of the oldest continuously operating inns in the US.

6 Norman Rockwell Museum

📍 Rte 9, Stockbridge
🕒 Wed, Thanksgiving, Dec 25 & 31 🌐 nrm.org
This museum was set up in 1969 to honor Normal Rockwell, whose works celebrate small-town

American life in the mid-20th century. Other exhibitions explore the work of modern illustrators.

7 Great Barrington

A vibrant mix of artists, artisans, business folk, and New Age visionaries makes Great Barrington the hippest town in the Berkshires, as well as a gateway to antiques shopping on Route 7.

8 Jacob's Pillow Dance Festival

📍 358 George Carter Rd, Becket
🌐 jacobspillow.org
This woodsy mountaintop retreat in Becket serves as the venue for performances by world-famous dance troupes.

9 Lenox

A hub for luxury shopping and performing arts, this village is surrounded by grand houses and vast estates.

MOHAWK TRAIL

Opened in 1914, the Mohawk Trail (*p62*) is one of the oldest scenic and tourist routes in the US. However, its history dates back much further. The route was originally carved out by Indigenous peoples. Early settlers from Europe later used it to travel between Boston and New York, adapting the path to suit their transport (horse and wheel).

10 North Adams

Originally an industrial R&D center during World War II, North Adams town is now a hub for arts and culture. It is best known for Mass MoCA (*p48*), the largest contemporary visual and performing arts center in the US.

Clockwise from right **The Red Lion Inn, Stockbridge; a laundry room in Hancock Shaker Village; exterior of the Norman Rockwell Museum; Mount Greylock's summit**

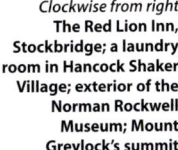

MOUNT DESERT ISLAND, MAINE

📍 R3

Home to Acadia National Park, Mount Desert Island blends Maine's fabled coast and woods into one magical spot. The island's southwest features salt-splashed fishing villages, while Bar Harbor on the east bustles with hotels and restaurants. Its beauty, depicted by 19th-century painters, inspired the rich to build summer estates here.

1 Bass Harbor Head Light Station

At the southern tip of Mount Desert, this lighthouse marks the entrance to Maine's Bass Harbor, offering stunning views of the blue ocean. In 1898, a 4,000-pound (1,800-kg) bell was added.

2 Southwest Harbor

Tucked inside two lobes of Mount Desert Island, this harbor is delightfully tranquil and picturesque. Its offshore waters are often filled with vessels crafted by the famed yacht-builders Hinckley and Morris. Visitors can enjoy a lobster-hauling boat ride or catch the seasonal Cranberry Isles ferry from here.

3 Bar Harbor

This lively resort town on Frenchman Bay is known for the grand mansions that line its shore. It serves as a tourist center for the island and a convenient base for exploring Acadia National Park (nps.gov/acad).

Bass Harbor Head Light Station

Entrance to the Abbe Museum, Bar Harbor

8 Jordan Pond House

🚗 R3 🏠 Park Loop Rd, 🕐 Jun–Sep: 11am–9pm daily 🌐 jordanpond house.com

For a touch of gentility in the wilderness, nothing beats sitting on the grassy lawn of the Jordan Pond House, where you can enjoy the famous popovers with afternoon tea.

4 Abbe Museum

Explore 10,000 years of Indigenous culture in this Bar Harbor museum *(p134)* devoted to the heritage of the Wabanaki peoples. Displays feature basketry and wood carving.

TOP TIP

For visits to Acadia National Park *(nps. gov/acad)*, reserve lodgings well in advance.

---

5 Cadillac Mountain

It's worth rising early to hike or drive up the 1,527-ft (465-m) Cadillac Mountain to catch the sunrise from the highest point on the eastern seaboard of the US.

6 Sand Beach

This 870-ft (265-m) stretch of sandy cove is perfect for sunbathing and swimming, though ocean waters rarely exceed 55º F (15º C).

7 Thunder Hole

Strong waves crash against the craggy ledges here, forcing air and water into a deep crevice beneath the rock, which, under favorable conditions, creates a ground-shaking thunderclap.

9 Carriage Roads

To preserve car-free tranquility, John D. Rockefeller Jr. built 45 miles (72 km) of carriage roads through land he gave to Acadia National Park – still reserved for hikers, cyclists, skiers, and equestrians.

10 Hiking Trails

To penetrate the deep wilderness or get up close and personal with the mountains of Acadia National Park, use the network of more than 150 miles (240 km) of trails. They range from easy to very strenuous.

WILDLIFE IN ACADIA NATIONAL PARK

Mount Desert Island is part of Acadia National Park, an area rich in wildlife. Hikers might spot white-tailed deer, red foxes, and woodchucks (groundhogs) amid the foliage. The area is also a haven for birdlife, with 338 bird species recorded, including owls, eagles, and peregrine falcons.

Hiking through Acadia National Park

PORTLAND AND CASCO BAY, MAINE

Maine's largest city, Portland lives by its motto, Resurgam, or "I shall rise again." The city has burned down four times since its foundation in 1633, resulting in a legacy of sturdy stone Victorian structures. Redevelopment has introduced a range of recreation options to its waterfront, and former warehouses have become boutiques and galleries. Just a short drive from downtown are the sandy beaches of Casco Bay.

Dining room at the Victoria Mansion

1 Victoria Mansion

📍 109 Danforth St, Portland 🕐 10am–4pm daily 🌐 victoriaman sion.org 🔗

Built in 1860, this elaborate Italianate mansion served as the summer home of Portland-born hotelier Sylvester Morse, who made his fortune in New Orleans. Its interior has striking decorative details, such as painted trompe l'oeil walls and ceilings, intricate wood paneling, and marble mantels.

2 Portland Museum of Art (PMA)

This fine-art museum (p48) occupies three buildings in Federal, Beaux Arts, and Postmodern styles. It features a collection of paintings by famous American painters W. Homer, Marsden Hartley, and Rockwell Kent.

3 Old Port District

The colorful shops of the Old Port District range from dealers in antiques and fine crafts to coffee roasters, candy stores, and boutiques. Both freshly caught lobsters and harbor-island commuters come ashore at the docks.

4 Portland Observatory

📍 138 Congress St
📞 207 774 5561 🔗

Built in 1807 to alert merchants to arriving ships, this 86-ft- (26-m-) tall observation tower is the last remaining US maritime signal station.

5 Hadlock Field

📍 271 Park Ave, Portland 📞 800 936 3647 🔗

Built in 1994, this Minor League Baseball stadium

Cobbled street in the Old Port District, Portland

Portland Head Light in Fort Williams Park

beach, go looking for shells, or take a dip to appreciate the safe waters: this local beach is beloved by locals, particularly families.

9 Two Lights State Park

🏛 Cape Elizabeth ▢

Sandy dunes and rocky points meet at this state park named for a pair of 19th-century lighthouses.

10 Windjammer and Whale-Watching Cruises

You might see humpback, finback, or minke whales roll in the water, spout, and leap during a whale-watching trip *(odyssey whalewatch.com)*, or enjoy a view of Portland skyline from Casco Bay on a sail aboard a sloop *(maine sailingadventure.net)*.

is home to the Portland Sea Dogs. It's named after baseball coach and Hall of Famer Edson B. Hadlock.

6 Children's Museum & Theater of Maine

🏛 250 Thompson's Point Rd ⏱ 9am–4pm Wed–Mon 🌐 hitetails.org

A must-visit for children under 12, this museum and theater has an ambitious program of interactive exhibits and plays designed to entertain and enlighten.

7 Fort Williams Park

🏛 Cape Elizabeth

One of the world's most photographed light-houses, Portland Head,

in Fort Williams Park, is also Maine's oldest lighthouse. Completed in 1791, it marks the entrance to Casco Bay.

8 Crescent Beach State Park

🏛 Cape Elizabeth ▢

Spread out a blanket on the mile-long arc of

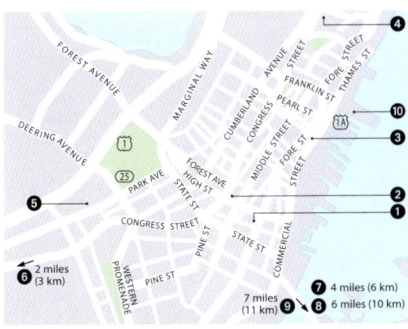

WHITE MOUNTAINS, NEW HAMPSHIRE

📍 L3–L4 & M3–M4

Over 48 peaks have come to define the rugged north country of New Hampshire, a large part of which is the White Mountain National Forest. The area is ideal for hiking and fall foliage sightseeing: drive through to witness tumbling waterfalls, deep glens, and dark forests. Wildlife abounds – be careful of deer and moose on the roads at dusk.

1 Whale's Tale Waterpark

📍 481 Daniel Webster Hwy, Lincoln ⏱ Hours vary, chech website 🌐 whalestalewater park.net ↗

New Hampshire's top aquatic attraction, this 17-acre (7-ha) waterpark features water slides for every age, wave pools, wading pools, and a river that snakes through the park.

2 Franconia Notch State Park

📍 Flume Gorge, Daniel Webster Hwy, Lincoln 📞 603 823 800 ⏱ Mid-May–mid-Oct ↗

This 8-mile- (13-km-) long mountain pass between the Franconia and

Kinsman mountain ranges is known for its rock walls and waterfalls and the challenging trails of the Flume Gorge.

3 Lincoln and Woodstock

With the Kancamagus Highway to the east and Franconia Notch to the north, Lincoln and Woodstock are two

charming villages that serve as base camps for outdoors enthusiasts.

4 Kancamagus Highway

One of few roads across the spine of the White Mountains, the 34-mile (55-km) "Kanc" is among the state's most thrilling drives (p62). Park at designated areas to picnic, hike along streams, or visit settlement sites.

TOP TIP

In foliage season, drive the "Kanc" on a weekday, when there's less traffic.

Lush foliage in Franconia Notch State Park

Heritage Cog Railway, Mount Washington

5 Conway Scenic Railroad

Enjoy the mountain scenery from an old-fashioned train *(p62)* as it travels through Mount Washington Valley or over the towering trestles of Crawford Notch.

6 North Conway

Gateway to the east side of the White Mountains, North Conway is a bustling commercial center. Spend the morning hiking and the afternoon browsing for bargain designer goods.

7 Mount Washington and the Cog Railway

🏠 Marshfield Base Station, off Rte 302
🌐 thecog.com ↗

New England's highest mountain peak at 6,288 ft (1,917 m), Mount Washington has lured climbers and sightseers since the 1840s. For the most picturesque ascent, take a three-hour round trip on the Cog Railway, operating since 1869.

8 Mount Washington Hotel and Resort

🏠 310 Mt Washington Hotel Rd, Bretton Woods
🌐 omnihotels.com

Opened in 1902, this White Mountain resort is renowned for its legendary golf and winter skiing.

9 Pinkham Notch

🏠 Joe Dodger Lodge, Rte 16, north of North Conway 📞 603 466 2727

This rocky pass is a hub for skiers and hikers. Hikes range from easy walks to rigorous trails.

10 Ski Mountains

With their dramatic drops and heavy snowfall, the White Mountains are a top ski destination. For the best range of down-hill runs, head to Bretton Woods, Cannon Mountain *(p64)*, Wildcat Mountain, and Loon Mountain.

APPALACHIAN TRAIL

Following the leafy Appalachian Mountains from Maine down to Atlanta, the AT *(appalachiantrail.org)* is one of the most legendary hiking trails in the US. It passes through most of New England's states and ticks off both the White Mountains and the Green Mountains *(p40)* along the way. Seek out a section, or, if you're up for the challenge, take on the entire trail.

LAKES REGION, NEW HAMPSHIRE

📍 M4–M5

The stunning lakes dotting the vicinity of the White Mountains began drawing settlers in the mid-18th century. Roads and railroads proliferated here in the 19th century, opening New Hampshire's lakes to tourism. Since then, tourists have flocked here for watersports, scenic hiking, quaint resort towns, and sandy beaches.

1 Lake Winnipesaukee

At 21 miles (34 km) long, Winnipesaukee is New Hampshire's largest lake. Swimmers love to congregate on its pine-rimmed beaches, while some race motorboats and hold water-skiing contests.

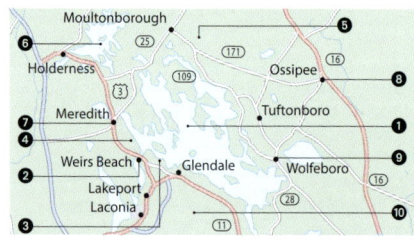

2 Weirs Beach

Vacationers swarm this brassy resort on the west end of Lake Winnipesaukee, where the beach and boardwalk are augmented by fairground rides, a water slide, mini-golf, souvenir shops, and an abundance of cotton-candy stores.

3 M/S Mount Washington

🕐 Late-May–mid-Oct
🌐 cruisenh.com 📲

Cruising on this 230-ft- (70-m-) historic vessel

is the best way to see Lake Winnipesaukee. Along the way, listen to a running commentary on celebrity homes and other attractions.

4 Winnipesaukee Scenic Railroad

🏠 154 Main St, Meredith 🕐 May–Oct 🌐 gsscenic. com 🔗

You never lose sight of Winnipesaukee on summer shoreline excursions between Meredith and Lakeport, with stopovers at Weirs Beach. The railroad also runs weekend fall foliage trips.

5 Castle in the Clouds

🏠 Moultonborough 🕐 Mid-May–mid-Oct: daily 🌐 castleinthe clouds.org 🔗

Set on a bluff 750 ft (229 m) above Lake Winnipesaukee, this

Moultonborough's Castle in the Clouds

historic stone castle features 28 miles (45 km) of hiking trails, and a pretty waterfall.

6 Squam Lake

Best known as the setting for the 1981 movie *On Golden Pond*, Squam is a natural paradise, best appreciated on a boat with a guide from the Squam Lakes Natural Science Center *(nhnature.org)*.

7 Meredith

An upscale resort town on Lake Winnipesaukee, Meredith is famous for its warm-water bass fishing and serves as the lake's primary shopping destination.

8 Ossipee

Set in a pond-dotted plateau just east of Lake Winnipesaukee, Ossipee is perfect for hiking, blackberry picking, and horseback riding on quiet country roads.

Houses alongside Lake Winnipesaukee

9 Wolfeboro

A resort town since 1769 and the largest community on the lake, Wolfeboro represents the gentrified side of Winnipesaukee.

10 Gunstock Mountain Resort

🏠 719 Cherry Valley Rd, Gilford 🕐 Hours vary, chech website 🌐 gun stoch.com 🔗

Originally a Depression-era public-works project, Gunstock is now a ski area, and its forests draw outdoor enthusiasts.

MOTORCYCLE WEEK

Tens of thousands of motorcycle enthusiasts gather in and around Laconia in mid-June for the adrenaline-charged races of the Laconia Motorcycle Week, an annual event since 1925. Area lodging books up in advance.

LITCHFIELD HILLS, CONNECTICUT

📍 B4–B5

Tucked into the northwest corner of Connecticut, the undulating Litchfield Hills are the most scenic and bucolic section of the state. Most towns nestle in the Housatonic River valley, and their historic homes attest to its colonial past. The region is also laced with a network of mountain streams, making fly-fishing for trout a top activity.

1 Litchfield

This eponymous market town is a popular base in the Litchfield Hills. Locals flock here to shop, dine, worship, and admire the many historic homes, including the first US law school (1784).

2 Woodbury

With its many shops and dealers, this is a popular haunt for antiques lovers. In the village center, check out late 18th-century style at the historic Glebe House Museum *(p106)*, which showcases period furniture in situ.

🍴 **EAT**

Indulge in farm-based cuisine at the Good News Restaurant *(p110)* in Woodbury.

3 Housatonic River

As the Housatonic River nears the covered bridge at West Cornwall, it enters a 12-mile (19-km) stretch that many rank the best fly-fishing in eastern US. Join sportspeople from New England trying their luck here in the spring.

4 Lake Waramaug

Farmland around New Preston's Lake Waramaug is temperate enough to grow wine grapes. Stop by Hopkins Vineyard to sample the vintages. A state park on the broad, scenic lake offers picnic grounds, swimming, and fishing.

5 Institute for American Indian Studies (IAIS)

🏠 38 Curtis Rd, Washington 🕐 11am–4pm Thu–Sun 🌐 iais museum.org ❂

Tucked high into the woods of Washington, this facility re-creates a pre-European-contact Algonkian village. With a collection of artifacts dating back 10,000 years, it's the perfect spot to learn about the Indigenous culture of northwestern Connecticut.

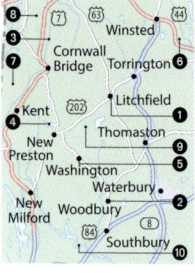

Covered West Cornwall Bridge

Tubers floating down the Farmington River

NEIGHBORS WITH NAMES

The combination of Litchfield Hills' natural beauty and its easy proximity to New York City conspire to make it the home of many celebrities. Among the residents over the years have been sculptor Alexander Calder, chef Jacques Pepin, author William Styron, and a number of actors, including Meryl Streep.

6 Farmington River Tubing

☐ 92 Main St, New Hartford ☐ Hours vary, chech website ⊎ farmingtonrivertubing.com ☑

Spend a summer afternoon leisurely floating down the Farmington River on an inflatable tube. The 2.5-mile (4-km) course takes in gentle ripples and a segment of turbulent rapids.

7 Kent Falls State Park

☐ Rte 7, Kent ☐ 860 927 3238 ☑

North of the village of Kent, this park is home to an impressive waterfall, a 250-ft (76-m) drop over slate and marble. Follow the trail to the top to see the most vigorous chute of all.

8 Lime Rock Park

☐ 60 White Hollow Rd, Lakeville ☐ Hours vary, chech website ⊎ limeroch.com ☑

Lime Rock Park is home to a 1.5-mile (2.4-km) race track where major racing events are held, featuring stock cars, road racers, and formula vehicles. The park also offers high-speed driving classes.

9 Mount Tom State Park

☐ Rte 202, Litchfield ☐ 8am–sunset daily ☑

At 500 ft (152 m), Mount Tom offers superb summit views. The park's lake is a favorite with families and scuba divers alike.

10 Shepaug Dam

In icy winter, more bald eagles congregate at the Shepaug Dam in Southbury than almost any other place in New England. Camouflaged blinds let birdwatchers get close-up views.

Bald eagle in flight, Shepaug Dam

GREEN MOUNTAINS, VERMONT

◎ K3–K6 & J6 ⓘ Green Mountain National Forest Manchester Ranger Station: 2538 Depot St, Manchester Center; fs.usda.gov

The Green Mountains form Vermont's north-south backbone, running from Quebec to Massachusetts. Much of this wilderness is preserved as the Green Mountain National Forest, attracting millions for fishing, hiking, mountain biking, camping, and skiing. State Route 100, spanning Green Mountains's east and west ranges, is famous for fall foliage.

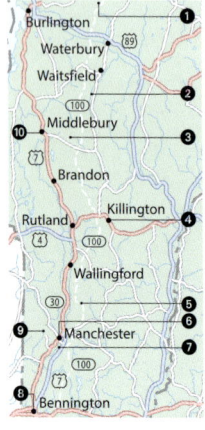

1 Stowe and Mount Mansfield

The von Trapps of *Sound of Music* fame settled in Stowe because it so resembled the Austrian Alps. Hikers and skiers flock to the village at the foot of Mount Mansfield.

2 Mad River Valley

Tucked between two ranges of the Green Mountains, this region includes a ski area *(p65)*, the chic Waitsfield village, and the outdoors sports center of Warren.

> **EAT**
> The Warren Store *(284 Main St, Warren)* serves hot grilled food – sandwiches, pastries, and sweets – for breakfast and lunch.

You'll also spot historic covered bridges crossing many rivers.

3 Robert Frost Wayside

Poet Robert Frost (1874–1963) and New

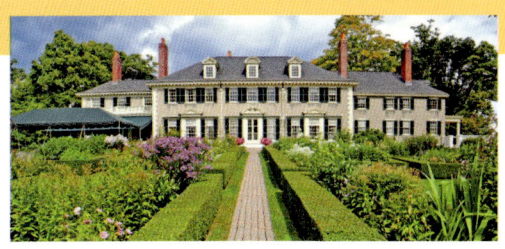

Clockwise from above
**Beautifully land-
scaped gardens
at Hildene house;
Bennington Battle
Monument; ski lift
and alpine slide
in Killington**

England farm country are inseparable. See nature through a poet's eyes by following the interpretive trail in Ripton to a cabin where he wrote much of his later verse.

4 Killington
At 4,241 ft (1,292 m) the "beast of the East," Killington (p64), is the second-highest peak in Vermont, and home to the largest ski resort in eastern North America.

5 The Long Trail
🅵 Green Mountain Club Visitor Center: 4711 Eaterbury-Stowe Rd; greenmountainclub.org
This 270-mile (432-km) hiking trail follows the Green Mountains as it traverses most of Vermont's highest peaks. Enjoy a day-hike between access points.

6 Manchester
A genteel vacation resort since the 1890s,

Verdant scenery in the Green Mountains

Manchester is a posh town with marbled sidewalks. Shop in the high-end designer outlet stores on the outskirts, or hit the slopes at the nearby Stratton and Bromley ski areas.

7 Hildene
🅰 1005 Hildene Rd, Manchester 🕙 10am–4:30pm Thu–Mon 🆆 hildene.org
This 412-acre (167-ha) Georgian Revival house was built for Robert Todd Lincoln, the diplomat son of US president Abraham Lincoln (1809–65). Highlights include family memorabilia, and a 1,000-pipe Aeolian organ. Some 12 miles (19 km) of surrounding trails entice hikers, snowshoers, and cross-country skiers.

8 Bennington
This town's main attraction is the Bennington Battle Monument (bennington battlemuseum.com) that honors an American Revolutionary War

victory. The Bennington Museum (p116) displays folk art and Americana.

9 Mount Equinox Skyline Drive
🅰 42 Skyline Dr, Arlington 🕙 Late-May–end-Oct: 9am–5pm daily 🆆 equinox mountain.com
This 5-mile (8-km) toll road, along a high ridge, offers superb sunsets and breathtaking views.

10 Middlebury
The archetypal New England town, Middlebury is known for its prestigious college, tall-spired churches, and collection of colonial-era homes. The town also hosts a number of old mill buildings along Otter Creek.

TOP TIP

Be prepared for road closures as temperatures dip in winter, spelling icy conditions.

NEWPORT, RHODE ISLAND

📍 F5 🎫 21 Long Wharf Mall; discovernewport.org

The small city of Newport packs a huge amount of history into a few square miles. America's first naval college and oldest synagogue are here, as is the White Horse Tavern, which has been operating since 1673. Other sights include its 19th-century mansions, built by the rich to flee the fetid summer of New York. The summer base of the New York Yacht Club, the city hosts many contenders for the America's Cup sailing race.

1 The Breakers

🏠 44 Ochre Point Ave 📞 401 847 6544 🕐 Hours vary, call ahead 🔗

This 70-room Italian Renaissance-style mansion, with its gilt- and marble-encrusted interior, offers a breath-taking insight into the pre-eminence of the Vanderbilt family, who were among America's economic aristocracy.

2 Cliff Walk

This exhilarating 3.5-mile (5.6-km) amble along Newport's east-facing cliffs will have you looking two ways – up to the lawns of the mansions on Bellevue Avenue, and down to watch surfers catching waves at Easton's Beach.

3 International Tennis Hall of Fame

🏠 194 Bellevue Ave 🕐 10am–5pm daily 🌐 tennisfame.com 🔗

Sports-loving visitors can play on the grass courts where US tournament tennis was born in 1881. The Hall still hosts professional matches, while its excellent museum chronicles the sport.

4 Touro Synagogue

🏠 85 Touro St 🕐 Hours vary, check website 🌐 touro synagogue.org 🔗

The oldest synagogue in America, the spare and elegant Touro Synagogue was con-structed in 1763 by religious refugees from Spain and Portugal. It's now a National Historic Site.

Sailboats at Newport Harbor

NEWPORT REGATTA

Usually held in mid-July, the Newport Regatta features racing in over 20 "One-Design" classes, where American boats compete against others with similar design. Sailing is only half the fun – the regatta is the highlight of the summer social season that starts at the marinas and spills over into the lively bars and restaurants.

5 Washington Square

Colonial-era Newport's focal point was damaged but not destroyed by the British during the American Revolution.

The first RI state house heads the square.

6 America's Cup Charters Cruises

⏰ May–Oct 🌐 americascupcharters.com ↗

Enjoy Newport Harbor's beauty from the deck of a racing yacht – you may get to take the wheel.

7 Bowen's Wharf

Bowen's Wharf (p99) has been the anchor of Newport's waterfront activity since 1760. Head here for sailing or power-boat tours, shopping at boutiques, or casual and fine dining.

8 Museum of Newport History

📍 127 Thames St
⏰ 10am–4pm daily
🌐 newporthistory.org

One of Newport's architectural treasures, the 18th-century Brick Store is now a museum featuring exhibits that

DRINK
Keep an eye out for a truck selling Del's Lemonade along the Thames Street or at the Fort Adams State Park.

chronicle the city's social and economic past.

9 Fort Adams State Park

📍 Harrison Ave
🌐 fortadams.org

The windy point between Newport Harbor and the Narragansett Bay East Passage is the best spot to watch racing sailboats. Newport's famous music festivals are held here.

10 Rose Island and Lighthouse

⏰ Mid-May–mid-Oct
🌐 roseisland.org ↗

This historic lighthouse is manned by volunteers. Expert paddlers kayak here for excellent birding.

Clockwise from right
Old Colony State House at the east end of Washington Square; Rose Island Lighthouse; exhibits at the Touro Synagogue; Newport's scenic Cliff Walk

TOP 10 OF EVERYTHING

HISTORIC SITES

1 Old Sturbridge Village, MA

▣ D3 ▣ Rte 20, Sturbridge ▣ Early Apr–Sep: 9:30am–5pm Wed–Sun; Oct & Nov: 9:30am–4pm Wed–Sun Ⓦ osv.org ▣

This living history museum, the largest of its kind in New England, offers a vivid sense of 19th-century New England rural life. It features over 40 historic buildings, moved from across the region, along with heritage livestock breeds and costumed guides.

2 Strawbery Banke, NH

▣ N6 ▣ 14 Hancock St, Portsmouth ▣ Hours vary, chech website Ⓦ strawberybanke.org ▣▣

Situated near Portsmouth's vibrant waterfront district is the 10-acre (4-ha) site of Strawbery Banke, the city's original settlement. This complex of historic dwellings chronicles daily life in the seaside city from the 17th to the 20th century, with 17 rooms featuring period furnishings, and many historical gardens. Here, costumed guides bring more than 350 years of Portsmouth's history to life with tours, demonstrations, and workshops.

3 Minute Man National Historical Park, MA

▣ E2 ▣ Concord ▣ Dawn–dusk daily Ⓦ nps.gov/mima

This historic park commemorates the opening battle of the American Revolution on April 19, 1775, when British troops clashed with colonial rebels in Lexington and Concord. This pivotal event forced a British retreat and inspired other colonies to join the fight. The park preserves the

The Minute Man by Daniel C. French

original battle sites where the historic clash took place and tells the story of the American militia, known as Minute Men. Its visitor center (*174 Liberty St; 978 318 7810*) features a battle mural and a 27-minute multimedia show.

4 Billings Farm and Museum, VT

▣ K5 ▣ 69 Old River Rd, Woodstock ▣ May–Oct: 10am–5pm daily; Nov–Feb: 10am–4pm Sat & Sun Ⓦ billings farm.org ▣▣

Set up in 1871, Billings Farm was turned into a museum of rural life in 1983. Its rolling green pastures and fine farm buildings represent the ideal of Vermont dairy farming. Visitors will get an opportunity to interact with sheep, horses, and chickens, and watch the herd of Jersey cows being milked. The farm also hosts ploughing competitions in the spring and apple-cider pressing in the fall.

5 Plimoth Patuxet, MA

▣ G3 ▣ 137 Warren Ave, Plymouth ▣ Mar–Nov: 9am–5pm daily Ⓦ plimoth.org ▣▣

Founded in 1947, this living museum chronicles the lives of the 17th-century English settlers in Plymouth, and the Indigenous peoples (such as the Wampanoag culture) who came before them. The museum features costumed interpreters who narrate the history of this town and its people.

6 Hancock Shaker Village, MA

▣ B2 ▣ 1843 W Housatonic St, Rte 20, Pittsfield ▣ Mid-Apr–Jun: 11am–4pm daily; late Jul–Oct: 10am–5pm daily; Nov: 11am–4pm Fri–Sun Ⓦ hancock shakervillage.org ▣

Dating from 1790, this settlement showcases the artful skills of the Shakers, an egalitarian Christian group founded in the 18th century. Its iconic

Round Stone Barn at the Hancock Shaker Village

1826 Round Stone Barn perfectly encapsulates their ability for making things both functional and beautiful.

7 Slater Mill, RI

E4 ◻ 67 Roosevelt Ave, Pawtucket ◻ Mid-May–mid-Oct: 10am–4pm Thu–Sun ◻ nps.gov/blrv ◻

Dating from 1793, Slater Mill was the first successful cotton-spinning mill in the US. The ingenuity of the early machinery, which was driven by hydro-power transmitted through giant flapping leather belts, will fascinate engineering buffs. Tours are held twice a week; check the website for details, and call ahead *(401 725 8638)* to book.

8 Canterbury Shaker Village, NH

M5 ◻ 288 Shaker Rd, Canterbury ◻ shakers.org ◻

Founded in 1792, Canterbury was a working Shaker village into the 1960s. Demonstrations and workshops teach visitors about Shaker skills and ideals, while daily tours of original Shaker buildings include anecdotes of the last generation of Shakers to live here.

9 Weir Farm National Historic Site, CT

B6 ◻ 735 Nod Hill Rd, Wilton ◻ May–Oct: 10am–4pm Wed–Sun ◻ nps.gov/wefa

The painter J. Alden Weir (1852–1919) made this rustic farm into a retreat for himself and his friends at the end of the 19th century. Two more generations of artists worked here before the property passed into the care of the National Park Service. The grounds are open daily from dawn to dusk.

10 Lowell National Historical Park, MA

F2 ◻ Lowell ◻ Late Apr–May: noon–5pm Mon–Fri; Jun–Oct: 10am–5pm daily ◻ nps.gov/lowe ◻

The birthplace of the Industrial Revolution in the US, Lowell is home to an urban park that preserves the city's intricate network of canals and several 19th-century textile mills. The sight of the mighty water-powered looms operating in the 1864 Boott Cotton Mill gives a real sense of what it was like to work here. To learn more about the area's history and to participate in ranger-guided tours of the mills as well as the canals, stop by the park's visitor center *(246 Market St, 978 970 5000)*.

Artworks on display at the Wadsworth Atheneum

ART MUSEUMS

1 Wadsworth Atheneum, Hartford, CT
C4 600 Main St Noon–5pm Thu–Sun thewadsworth.org

Established in 1842, the Wadsworth Atheneum is the oldest public art museum in the US. It houses New England's best collection of the startlingly oversized landscapes of the Hudson River School, alongside notable Baroque pieces and French and American Impressionist paintings.

2 Mass MoCA, North Adams, MA
B2 1040 Mass MoCA Way 10am–5pm Wed–Mon mass moca.org

The Mass MoCA museum focuses on work by contemporary artists, and also stages dance, avant-garde theater, and performance art.

3 Portland Museum of Art, Portland, ME
N4 7 Congress Sq 10am–6pm Tue–Sun (to 8pm Fri) portlandmuseum.org

Maine's largest art museum, the Portland Museum of Art features works of major landscape painters such as Marsden Hartley and Fitz Henry Lane. Tours of the Winslow Homer studio on Prouts Neck are run from May to mid-November.

4 Worcester Art Museum, MA
E3 55 Salisbury St 10am–4pm Wed–Sun worcesterart.org

Striking Roman mosaics, arms and armor, and a top collection of pre-Columbian art from Mexico and Central America are the highlights at this general art museum.

5 Currier Museum of Art, Manchester, NH
M6 150 Ash St 10am–5pm Wed–Sun currier.org

This museum is home to an excellent collection of European and contemporary art. It also owns the nearby Zimmerman House and Kalil House, both designed in the 1950s by pioneering American architect Frank Lloyd Wright as an exemplar of his Usonian homes. Both houses are open to the public through guided tours.

6 Museum of Fine Arts, Boston, MA
S6 465 Huntington Ave 10am–5pm Mon, Wed, Sat & Sun, 10am–10pm Thu & Fri mfa.org

Highlights at Boston's world-class Museum of Fine Arts (MFA) include major holdings of Asian, Egyptian, and Nubian art. It also has the most important Monet collection outside of Paris.

7 Peabody Essex Museum, Salem, MA

⬕ F2 ⬕ East India Sq ⬕ 10am–5pm Thu–Mon ⬕ pem.org ⬕

This glass-and-brick building is filled with a staggering collection of artworks, furniture, and artifacts, from East and South Asia, Oceania, and Indigenous American communities.

8 The Clark, Williamstown, MA

⬕ B2 ⬕ 225 South St ⬕ Jul & Aug: 10am–5pm daily; Sep–Jun: 10am–5pm Tue–Sun ⬕ clarkart.edu ⬕

Housed in a Postmodern building, this museum's collection focuses on French Impressionists and English landscape artists. It serves as a multidisciplinary research institute for art history, too.

9 Shelburne Museum, VT

⬕ J3 ⬕ Rte 7, Shelburne ⬕ Hours vary, check website ⬕ shelburnemuseum.org ⬕

From elaborately stitched quilts to two miniature circuses, this museum celebrates American folk art and ingenuity.

10 Isabella Stewart Gardner Museum, Boston, MA

⬕ S6 ⬕ 25 Evans Way ⬕ 11am–5pm Wed–Mon (to 9pm Thu), 10am–5pm Sat & Sun ⬕ gardnermuseum.org ⬕

One of the all-time great private collectors, Gardner built this lovely Renaissance-style palace to display her 2,500-object collection.

Courtyard at the Isabella Stewart Gardner Museum

TOP 10
ARTISTS OF NEW ENGLAND

Sculptor Louise Nevelson

1. John Singleton Copley (1738–1815)
The first great portraitist in the US. Copley fled to England during the Revolution.

2. Fitz Henry Lane (1805–65)
Gloucester-based Lane revolutionized the handling of light in seascapes.

3. Winslow Homer (1836–1910)
Homer is most celebrated for his vigorous Maine seascapes.

4. Childe Hassam (1859–1935)
Hassam skillfully depicted both New England cityscapes and countryside.

5. Marsden Hartley (1877–1943)
Hartley's abstract landscapes were inspired by his native Maine.

6. Edward Hopper (1882–1967)
Hopper's seascapes are notable for their psychological depth.

7. Louise Nevelson (1899–1988)
Nevelson is known for her great Abstract Expressionist assemblages.

8. Corita Kent (1918–86)
A nun who became a graphic artist, Kent emphasized social justice in her Pop Art, including *Rainbow Gas*, a Boston landmark.

9. John Woodrow Wilson (1922–2015)
Lithographer, sculptor, and painter, Boston-born Wilson was known for his racially and politically charged art.

10. Molly Neptune Parker (1939–2020)
Neptune is famous for reviving the art of Passamaquoddy basketry.

UNIVERSITY MUSEUMS

1 Smith College Museum of Art, Northampton, MA

🅟 C3 🏛 20 Elm St 🕐 11am–4pm Tue–Sun 🆆 scma.smith.edu

Since its founding in the 1870s, Smith has amassed over 27,000 works from cultures around the world to make up this teaching collection. A 1943 Rufino Tamayo mural fills the museum's atrium.

2 Yale University Art Museums, New Haven, CT

🅟 C5 🏛 Chapel St

The largest collection of British art outside the UK is housed at the Yale Center for British Art (*britishart.yale. edu*), designed by modernist architect Louis B. Kahn. The Yale University Art Gallery (*artgallery.yale.edu*), an earlier Kahn building of 1953, is noted for its extensive collection of Asian, African, European, American, and pre-Columbian art. Among its prized American pieces is John Trumbull's 1786 painting of the battle of Bunker Hill. It also houses works by Picasso, Van Gogh, and Monet.

3 Harvard Art Museums, Cambridge, MA

🅟 F2 🏛 32 Quincy St 🕐 10am–5pm Tue–Sun 🆆 harvardart museums.org 🔗

One of the world's most wide-ranging university art museums, this complex brings together three principal museums: the Fogg Art, BuschReisinger, and Arthur M. Sackler galleries. Its outstanding collections include ancient Greek, medieval, Renaissance, Impressionist, Expressionist, and Asian art.

Bodhisattva statue, Harvard Art Museums

4 Hood Museum of Art, Hanover, NH

🅟 L4 🏛 Dartmouth College 🕐 11am–5pm Wed, 11am–8pm Thu & Fri, 1–5pm Sat 🆆 hoodmuseum. dartmouth.edu

Operated by Dartmouth College, this gallery space has more than 65,000 artworks and photographs, which showcase a diverse collection that includes early American and European paintings, and works by such noted modern artists as Picasso. Highlights include Assyrian stone reliefs, while selections of Asian sub-Saharan, and Indigenous art provide a global perspective.

5 Peary-MacMillan Arctic Museum, Brunswick, ME

🅟 P4 🏛 Gibbons Center for Arctic Studies, Bowdoin College 🕐 10am–5pm Tue–Sat, 1–5pm Sun 🆆 bowdoin. edu/arctic-museum

Named for American explorers and Bowdoin College alumni Robert E. Peary and Donald B. MacMillan, this museum brings their daring Arctic explorations to life with natural history specimens, Inuit artifacts, and photographs.

6 Colby College Museum of Art, Waterville, ME

P3 5600 Mayflower Hill Dr 10am–5pm Tue–Sat, noon–5pm Sun museum.colby.edu

An excellent survey of major American artists is capped with holdings of contemporary artists associated with Maine, such as Marsden Hartley and Alex Katz.

7 Ballard Institute and Museum of Puppetry, Storrs, CT

D4 1 Royce Circle, Suite 101B, University of Connecticut Hours vary, chech website bimp.uconn.edu

This unique puppetry museum, one of America's largest, is home to the puppets of Frank Ballard, a drama professor who set up the country's first degree course in puppetry.

8 RISD Museum, Providence, RI

E4 20 N Main St 10am–5pm Tue, Wed & Fri–Sun, noon–8pm Thu risdmuseum.org

The RISD's historically encyclopedic collection of more than 100,000 objects is notable for late-19th-century paintings (including French Impressionist works), as well as post-1960 arts

Blaschka glass flowers, Harvard Museum of Natural History

in various media. Early American furniture stars in the decorative arts wing.

9 Harvard Museum of Natural History, Cambridge, MA

F2 26 Oxford St 9am–5pm daily hmnh.harvard.edu

This renowned museum combines the charm of old-fashioned artifacts with cutting-edge science. Its most famous attraction is the Glass Flowers exhibit, showcasing a collection of delicately and realistically re-created plants and blossoms by the father-and-son duo of Czech glass artists Leopold and Rudolf Blaschka. Dinosaur skeletons, gemstones, and meteorites are particularly popular with children.

10 Hudson Museum at University of Maine, Orono, ME

2 Flagstaff Rd 9am–4pm Mon–Fri umaine.edu/hudson

This fascinating museum has a dedicated section for ethnographic and archaeological Indigenous artifacts. The Penobscot basketry collection is the museum's prize display and ranks among the best in the world. Periodic workshops and exhibitions are held by leading Indigenous artists.

PERSONAL MUSEUMS

1 John F. Kennedy Presidential Library and Museum, Boston, MA

🅟 F3 🅐 Columbia Point 🅞 10am–5pm daily 🆆 jfklibrary.org ☑

This museum not only chronicles JFK's 1,000 days in office, it also touches on the man behind the myth.

2 Orchard House, Concord, MA

🅟 E2 🅐 399 Lexington Rd 🅞 Hours vary, chech website 🆆 louisamayalcott.org ☑

American novelist Louisa May Alcott not only set her 1868 classic *Little Women* in Orchard House, she also wrote it here. Now a museum to the author, the house is incredibly well preserved; even its interiors are as they were in the 1800s.

3 Mark Twain House, Hartford, CT

🅟 C4 🅐 351 Farmington Ave 🅞 9:30am–5:30pm daily 🕒 Jan–Mar: Tue 🆆 marktwainhouse.org ☑

Author Mark Twain lived in this 25-room home from 1874 to 1891 and penned seven books here. Designed by architect Edward Tuckerman Potter, the house is a masterpiece of American High Gothic style and features Tiffany interiors. The adjoining museum has exhibits on Twain and his contemporaries.

Iconic Mark Twain House in Hartford

4 Saint-Gaudens National Historic Site, Cornish, NH

🅟 L5 🅐 Rte 12A 🅞 Late May–Oct: 9am–4:30pm daily 🆆 nps.gov/saga ☑

This national historic site celebrates the life of Augustus Saint-Gaudens, America's leading sculptor of the Beaux-Arts generation. The house museum evokes the rustic idyll of the art colony that grew up around the sculptor, while its formal gardens feature a number of his sculptures.

5 Robert Frost Farm, Derry, NH

🅟 M6 🅐 122 Rockingham Rd 🅞 Hours vary, chech website 🆆 robertfrostfarm.org ☑

Young poet Robert Frost found his voice while living here from 1900 to 1911, and began writing the verse set in the New England countryside that would win him four Pulitzer Prizes.

6 Chesterwood, Stockbridge, MA

🅟 B3 🅐 4 Williamsville Rd 🅞 10am–5pm Wed–Mon 🆆 chesterwood.org ☑

The home and studio of Daniel Chester French, Chesterwood features the working models for his famous *Seated Lincoln* (1922), which would become Washington DC's famous Lincoln Memorial. The models remain in the studio, along with other plaster casts. During the summer months, the grounds are used to exhibit sculpture.

Dining room at Edith Wharton's summer home, The Mount

7 The Mount, Lenox, MA

🗺 B3 📍 2 Plunkett St 🕐 Early May–Oct: 10am–5pm daily 🌐 edithwharton.org ♿

This beautiful Berkshires estate dates from 1902 and showcases the design and decorating sensibilities of literary giant Edith Wharton.

8 Longfellow House–Washington's Headquarters National Historic Site, Cambridge, MA

🗺 F2 📍 105 Brattle St 🕐 Late May–Oct: 9:30am–5pm Fri–Mon 🌐 nps.gov/long

The home of poet Henry Wadsworth Longfellow, one of America's influential literary figures, lays bare both his triumphs and tragedies, such as the fire that killed his wife and scarred his face, making him grow his signature beard.

9 Farnsworth Art Museum, Rockland, ME

🗺 Q3 📍 16 Museum St 🕐 Hours vary, chech website 🌐 farnsworthmuseum.org ♿

This museum showcases artists inspired by Maine's landscape. Its Wyeth Center celebrates the art dynasty of American artists N. C., Andrew, and James Wyeth.

10 Gropius House, Lincoln, MA

🗺 F2 📍 68 Baker Bridge Rd 🕐 11am–4pm Thu–Sun (Nov–Apr: Sat & Sun only) 🌐 historicnewengland.org ♿

One of the 20th century's most influential architects, Walter Gropius designed this unique home in 1937 by combining traditional New England materials with innovative modern elements such as chrome banisters and acoustical plaster.

TOP 10
NEW ENGLAND BOOKS

1. Hotel New Hampshire by John Irving
A tale of despair and redemption at an old resort hotel.

2. Country of the Pointed Firs by Sarah Orne Jewett
A psychological novel about women in rural Maine, first published 1896.

3. Outermost House by Henry Beston
An account of a year living on Cape Cod's Great Beach.

4. American Primitive by Mary Oliver
This Pulitzer Prize-winning collection covers love and nature on Cape Cod.

5. Walden by Henry David Thoreau
Thoreau's philosophical musings in the Massachusetts woods remain a key text in American thought.

6. Mystic River by Dennis Lehane
Lehane's noir fiction reveals seamy undercurrents of life in South Boston.

7. Empire Falls by Richard Russo
Class-bound fatalism meets hope in a dying mill town in Maine in this novel.

8. Charlotte's Web by E. B. White
This children's classic finds philosophy in the barnyard.

9. The Wedding by Dorothy West
An intimate glimpse into African American middle class life on Martha's Vineyard in the 1950s.

10. Little Women by Louisa May Alcott
This literary classic follows the lives of the four March girls through childhood to adulthood.

Louisa May Alcott

Whale skeleton at the Nantucket Whaling Museum

MARITIME SITES

1 Nantucket Whaling Museum, Nantucket, MA

H5 **13 Broad St** **Hours vary, chech website** **nha.org**

For a century prior to the discovery of petroleum, Nantucket dominated the whaling industry with whale-oil lamps and candles. Today, the Nantucket Whaling Museum preserves this legacy. Partially set in a former whale-oil refinery and candle factory, this museum chronicles how this small island dominated the industry for nearly a century. Its collection features ship models, including a 28-ft (8-m) whaleboat, maps and charts, and a 46-ft (14-m) sperm whale skeleton.

2 Mystic Seaport, CT

D5 **75 Greenmanville Ave, Mystic** **Apr–Oct: 10am–5pm daily; Nov & Dec: 10am–4pm Thu–Sun** **mysticseaport.org**

This working replica of a 19th-century coastal village comprises more than 40 buildings open to the public, including a bank, chapel, tavern, ship-carver's studio, and schoolhouse where craftspeople practiced their trades. Visitors can walk the decks of historic vessels or see carpenters replank a vessel at a working shipyard here.

3 New Bedford Whaling National Historical Park, New Bedford, MA

F4 **33 William St** **Sunrise–sunset** **nps.gov/nebe**

In the 19th century, New Bedford was the world's leading whaling port. Many buildings of the era, including the Seamen's Bethel Chapel mentioned in Herman Melville's *Moby-Dick* (1851), have been preserved at this park. Don't miss the extraordinary scrim-shaw carvings and a half-scale whaling ship at the New Bedford Whaling Museum.

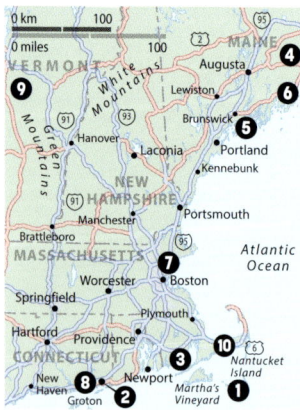

4 Penobscot Marine Museum, Searsport, ME

Q3 40 E. Main St Late-May–mid-Oct: 10am–5pm Tue–Sat penobscotmarinemuseum.org

Tiny Searsport was home to many of America's deep-water sea captains by the close of the 19th century. Recapture the adventure of that time with captains' chests from the China Trade, a whale's jaw, and a wall of portraits of some 300 Searsport sea captains.

5 Maine Maritime Museum, Bath, ME

P4 243 Washington St 9:30am–5pm daily mainemaritimemuseum.org

Ships have been built at the mouth of the Kennebec River for over three centuries. At Maine Maritime Museum, sail-era artifacts, paintings of historic vessels, and displays of Maine maritime life chronicle both the practicalities and the romance of that trade.

6 Maine Lighthouse Museum, Rockland, ME

Q3 1 Park Dr 10am–4pm daily mainelighthousemuseum.org

This is one of the world's largest collections of lighthouse artifacts. Marvel at gigantic prisms that made small lamps visible far out at sea, and learn how keepers lived.

7 Salem Maritime National Historic Site, Salem, MA

F2 2 New Liberty St 9:30am–4:30pm daily nps.gov/sama

This historic site explores Salem's oft-overlooked maritime history. At its peak, the town's harbor was a global trading center with around 50 wharves, where merchants would bring back riches from the Far East. Today, this bustling waterfront complex is home to three working wharves, including Derby Wharf, the longest of the three.

8 Historic Ship Nautilus and the Submarine Force Museum, Groton, CT

D5 1 Crystal Lake Rd 9am–4pm Wed–Mon ussnautilus.org

Located on the Thames River in Groton, this museum on the Naval Submarine Base is home to the USS *Nautilus*, the world's first nuclear-powered vessel and the first submarine to travel under the North Pole. Visitors can tour the vessel and even try commanding the sub at simulated controls.

9 Lake Champlain Maritime Museum, Vergennes, VT

J4 4472 Basin Harbor Rd Late May–mid-Oct: 10am–4pm daily lcmm.org

Relics from the more than 200 ships that have been wrecked on Lake Champlain are displayed here. Full-size working replicas of historic vessels help to bring the lake's boating history alive.

10 Whydah Pirate Museum, W. Yarmouth, MA

H4 674 MA-28 10am–5pm daily discoverpirates.com

Popular with youngsters, the Whydah Pirate Museum is named after "Black Sam" Bellamy's ship, *Whydah Gally*, which went down in a storm off Cape Cod in April 1717. This dockside display showcases discoveries from the ongoing excavations of the wreckage, uncovered in 1984, including a hoard of pirate treasure.

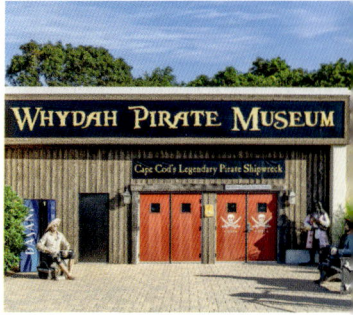

Entrance to the Whydah Pirate Museum in West Yarmouth

VILLAGES

1 Old Lyme, CT
◎ D5

If Old Lyme was not actually the cradle of American Impressionism, it was, at the very least the art movement's summer camp from 1899 into the 1930s. Surprisingly, little of either the landscape or the town has changed since that artistic heyday. Unlock the history with a visit to the Florence Griswold Museum (p106), where many of the artists lodged.

2 Tiverton Four Corners, RI
◎ F4

The crossroads at the center of rural Tiverton (p96), on the east side of Narragansett Bay, are lined with boutiques, antiques stores, and art galleries – all set in largely 18th-century buildings. The surrounding countryside is noted for its handsome historical stone walls and pastoral landscapes. The town also has arts and crafts galleries, a beloved ice-cream stand, and a gourmet store featuring local products.

3 Kingfield, ME
◎ N2

Gateway to the Sugarloaf ski resort, this characterful mountain village is popular with outdoors enthusiasts.

**Picturesque Sugarloaf
ski resort in Kingfield**

The Stanley Museum (stanleymuseum.org) here chronicles the achievements of twin native sons Francis Edgar and Freelan Oscar Stanley, best known for inventing the steam-powered Stanley Steamer cars. Their sister Chansonetta's documentary photographs capture rural life.

4 Watch Hill, RI
◎ E5

The gingerbread architecture of Westerly's seaside village of Watch Hill (p96) reveals its Victorian roots – there's even a Victorian tea room. Today, sport fishers come here for the perfect confluence of surf and shoreline currents.

5 Wethersfield, CT
◎ C4

Founded in 1634 as one of the three original settlements in Connecticut, Wethersfield is still home to some of the most striking colonial structures in the country – although admirers of architecture can get equally excited about the distinctive early 20th-century Hubbard Bungalows. The centerpiece is the Webb-Deane-Stevens Museum (p103), a trio of dwellings that illustrate the varied lifestyles of three Americans from the 18th century: a wealthy merchant, a diplomat, and a leather tanner. The museum also provides an interesting insight into the roots of the Colonial Revival movement in American style.

6 Wiscasset, ME

A thriving shipbuilding town in the 18th and 19th centuries, Wiscasset immodestly claims to be the "prettiest village in Maine." With baronial sea captains' homes that define the Federal style, a charming waterfront, and a generous sprinkling of boutiques and restaurants, it just might be. The 1807 Nickels-Sortwell House (*historicnewengland.org*), built for a wealthy ship owner, recaptures Wiscasset's glorious past.

7 New London, NH

Without the overhead power lines and asphalt on the roads, New London (*p104*) would look as if time had stopped around 1850. Home to Colby-Sawyer College, a prestigious liberal arts school, this lively town bustles during the summer as the shopping and dining center for Lake Sunapee vacationers; another draw is the Barn Playhouse's summer stock theater season.

8 Harrisville, NH
L6

A charming New England mill village, Harrisville is home to many picturesque structures including the 1838 general store, historic brick mills, and several wooden workers' cottages. It is the only early 19th-century industrial community in New England that is still perfectly preserved in its original form. Keen knitters will want to visit the yarn factory and store.

9 Grafton, VT

This genteel village bunched around the 1801 Grafton Inn epitomizes rustic Vermont charm. The Grafton Village Cheese Company (*p114*) makes top Vermont cheddars.

10 Shelburne Falls, MA
C2

Many artisans and musicians have built homes in this charming village on the Mohawk Trail (*p62*). The town is divided by the Deerfield River, which can be crossed via the Bridge of Flowers. The area gained fame centuries ago for its glacial potholes, carved by natural falls.

ISLANDS

1 Mount Desert Island, ME
Shaped like a baseball mitt, this big island is home to the summer resort town of Bar Harbor (p30) and the pristine paradise of Acadia National Park.

2 Nantucket Island, MA
Lying around 30 miles (48 km) off the southern tip of Cape Cod, Nantucket Island (p86) is a 14-mile-(22-km-) long enclave of tranquility. The island made its name through intrepid whaling and austere Quaker businessmen, who set the style with modest shingled homes. Its present-day attractions include pristine beaches, fascinating museums, and upscale shopping opportunities.

3 Block Island, RI
Between Long Island and the Rhode Island coast, this tiny island (p96) looks like a tintype of a Victorian resort. Its beaches, nature reserves, and historic lighthouses are best explored on a bike.

4 Isles of Shoals, NH
🅿 N6
These nine unforested rocky islands stand so far offshore that they were first used by English, Basque, and Breton anglers as camps to dry their catch in the summer sun. Visitors can book a narrated Isles of Shoals (isles ofshoals.com) and Portsmouth Harbor cruise to explore the islands. The trip also includes a walking tour of the Star Island, offering a glimpse into the isles' pirate history.

5 Monhegan Island, ME
🅿 Q4
Every seagull, twig, and moss-covered rock on Monhegan (p132) must have been depicted in an artwork over the century or so, ever since this fishing outpost off Maine became a summer art colony. Once the summer folk have gone, the anglers return.

6 Isle au Haut, ME
🅿 R4
A few miles from Stonington, this craggy rock offers all the attractions of Mount Desert Island but without the crowds. Almost half the island, about 4 sq miles (11 sq km), is part of Acadia National Park. Here, visitors can explore primeval bogs along its forested park trails and wild, wave-pounded bluffs, as well as enjoy numerous scenic hiking routes and stunning viewpoints.

7 Thimble Islands, CT
🅿 C6
Stories and legends abound about the Thimble Islands, a cluster of diminutive islets located just off the coast. On a narrated scenic cruise (thimbleisland cruise.com) you're very likely to hear a

Schooner Head on
Mount Desert Island

few of those tales, including the legend that the infamous pirate, Captain Kidd, buried treasure on Money Island. His gold hasn't been found to this day.

8 Boston Harbor Islands, MA
📍 F2 🕐 May–mid-Oct 🌐 boston harborislands.org

The Boston Harbor Islands have sandy hiking and nature trails, lifeguard-protected beaches, and a few old forts. You can reach the islands by ferry.

9 Plum Island, MA
📍 F1 🏠 Plum Island Turnpike, Newburyport 🌐 newburyport.com

This barrier island stretches 11 miles (18 km) south from Merrimack River and offers sandy beaches great for swimming. It is a wildlife refuge and home to several bird habitats.

10 Martha's Vineyard, MA
Locally known as "The Vineyard," this New England vacation island (p85) spans 108 sq miles (280 sq km), making it the largest in the region. It offers diverse attractions, from the elegant center of Edgartown and the distinctive gingerbread architecture of Oak Bluffs to the sacred clay cliffs revered by the Aquinnah Wampanoag community.

Gay Head Lighthouse
on Martha's Vineyard

TOP 10
LIGHTHOUSES

1. Sheffield Island
📍 B6 🏠 Norwalk Harbor, CT
Built in 1868, this fine lighthouse is located on the Norwalk Islands.

2. Stonington Harbor
📍 E5 🏠 7 Water St, Stonington, CT
Situated in a town rich in maritime history, the Granite Lighthouse now operates as a museum.

3. West Quoddy Head
📍 R2 🏠 Quoddy Head State Park, Lubec, ME
This iconic candy-striped light (1857) marks the easternmost point of the US.

4. Marshall Point
📍 Q4 🏠 Marshall Point Rd, Port Clyde, ME
Offshore light connected by a walkway to the keeper's house and museum.

5. Pemaquid Point
📍 P4 🏠 Off Rte 130, Bristol, ME
Built high on dramatic ledges in 1835, Pemaquid Point remains an essential navigational aid.

6. Portsmouth Harbor
📍 N6 🏠 Off Rte 1B, New Castle, NH
Built in 1878, this is the latest of several lighthouses built on New Castle island since 1771.

7. Beavertail
📍 E5 🏠 Beavertail State Park, Jamestown, RI
This is the third-oldest light on the eastern seaboard, built in 1783.

8. Highland
📍 H3 🏠 N. Truro, MA
Set atop a bluff at the Cape Cod National Seashore, this is the highest light on the New England mainland.

9. Nobska Point
📍 G5 🏠 Falmouth, MA
Sitting on the Shining Sea Bike Path, Nobska is visible for up to 16 miles (26 km).

10. Great Point
📍 H5 🏠 Nantucket Island, MA
Rebuilt in 1986 as a historic replica in the Coskata-Coatue Wildlife Refuge.

OCEAN BEACHES

1 Old Orchard Beach, Old Orchard, ME

N5

Old Orchard (*p132*) has been a popular resort beach since trains first ran here in 1842. A stretch of 3 miles (5 km) of the main beach guarantees plenty of room for sunbathing, swimming, kite-flying, and sandcastle-building. Stores, amusements, and rides ensure no one ever gets bored. During the summer there's a lively bar scene as well.

2 Hampton Beach, Hampton, NH

N6

Small, decorous state beaches dot Hampton's shoreline, but the main village beach is easily the most rau-cous, with outdoor concerts, sandcastle competitions, a flurry of summer activ-ities, and a stretch of souvenir stores and casual eateries. In summer the town is bilingual, reflecting its popu-larity with vacationers from Quebec. Swimmers and jet-skiers test the waters, parasailors soar overhead, and deep-sea fishing and whale-watching charter boats are available from Hampton Harbor.

3 Crane Beach, Ipswich, MA

G2

This 7-mile (11-km) stretch of copious white sand is one of New England's most picturesque swimming beaches. Carry binoculars as Crane is legendary for its diversity of bird species, although some nesting grounds may be off-limits between May and early August.

4 Misquamicut State Beach, Westerly, RI

E5 **riparks.ri.gov/beaches/misquamicut-state-beach**

Misquamicut (miss-KWAHM-i-cut) is one of New England's most popular family beaches, packing intense sum-mer entertainment into a relatively short stretch of white sand. Most rides, amusement stands, and food kiosks open from late June to August and also some fall weekends, but the beach is accessible all year. Parking lots fill early on summer weekends.

5 Hammonasset Beach State Park, Madison, CT

C5 **ctparks.com**

More than 2 miles (3 km) of brown sand beaches lapped by the gentle

Admiring the view from Hammonasset Beach State Park

Surfcasting at the Coast Guard Beach, Cape Cod

waves of Long Island Sound lure summer swimmers and sunbathers in droves, but Connecticut's longest shorefront park also has an excellent nature center at Meigs Point. Anglers stake out positions here early for excellent bluefish and striped bass fishing.

6 Salty Brine State Beach, Narragansett, RI

E5 W riparks.ri.gov/beaches/salty-brine-state-beach

With solar-powered, hot-water showers and electricity from wind turbines to supply the juice to recharge electric vehicles, this is the "greenest" beach facility in New England. The narrow strip of fine golden sand at the entrance to Galilee harbor has gentle waves, great views of fishing vessels, and some of the coast's finest seafood.

7 Old Silver Beach, Falmouth, MA

G4 W falmouthma.gov/151/Beach

This beautiful beach overlooking Buzzards Bay has warm summer waters, low waves, and a gradual drop-off, making it an ideal swimming spot for kids. Half the beach is reserved for Falmouth residents. Facing west over Buzzards Bay, Old Silver has some of New England's most scenic sunsets.

8 Coast Guard Beach, Eastham, MA

H4 W nps.gov/places/coast-guard-beach.htm

Arguably the best swimming beach on Cape Cod, Coast Guard Beach marks the beginning of the 30-mile (48-km) Great Beach of the Cape Cod National Seashore. A long and generous slope of sand leads down to the ocean, so the beach is rarely crowded. Stroll southward onto Nauset Spit to watch shore birds in summer and seals in winter.

9 Reid State Park, Georgetown, ME

P4 W maine.gov

Reid State Park beaches are long strands of brown sand backed by high dunes – the antithesis of the "rocky coast of Maine." Mile Beach and Half Mile Beach have lifeguards, changing rooms, and snack bars in summer. Visitors can swim safely along stretches sheltered from the ocean by sand bars, or break out the surf boards and head for more exposed parts of the beach.

10 Ogunquit Beach, Ogunquit, ME

N5

A 2-mile (3-km) cove lined with brown sand, Ogunquit Beach is well served by a summer trolley system that makes parking a cinch. The south end of the beach terminates at the romantic Marginal Way, a clifftop walking path through thickets of roses to the stores, restaurants, and copious art galleries of Perkins Cove. Its calm and clean waters, and the presence of many tide pools, make the beach a favorite with families.

Fall foliage on the Kancamagus Highwayl

WAYS TO SEE FOLIAGE

1 Kancamagus Highway, NH
📍M4 🌐hancamagushighway.com
Few foliage drives in New England match the thrill of hurtling along the "Kanc" through a tunnel of kaleidoscopic colors. This stretch of highway runs between Lincoln and Conway and covers about 34 miles (55 km) of Route 112.

2 Mohawk Trail, MA
📍B5
This historic Indigenous peoples' trade route over the Berkshire Hills (p28) follows the upper ranges of the Deerfield River – resplendent with acid-yellow alder and birch – until it climbs through fiery stands of maple, birch, and beech in the Charlemont State Forest. The drive ends by spiraling down the hillsides at the aptly named Hairpin Turn.

3 Conway Scenic Railroad, NH
📍M4 🏠38 Norcross Circle, N. Conway ⏱May–Nov 🌐conwayscenic.com ↗
There are several heritage train tours on offer along this railroad, but for the most striking foliage and close-up views of the Presidential Range in the White Mountains, take the Mountaineer train ride through Crawford Notch.

4 Lake Champlain Cruise, VT
📍J3 🏠Burlington Boathouse, 1 College St, Burlington ⏱Mid-May–mid-Oct 🌐soea.com ↗
Hop aboard the *Spirit of Ethan Allen III* for a guided cruise on Lake Champlain. While adults admire the verdant forests that surround the lake, kids eagerly look out for Champ, the legendary sea serpent that resides in the lake.

5 K-1 Gondola, VT
After a scenic gondola ride to the highest lift-served terrain in Vermont, a short, easy hike brings you to the summit of Killington Peak (p64) for a panoramic view of five states and part of Canada.

6 Essex Steam Train and Riverboat, CT
Combine a trip through the woods in restored 1920s railcars (p107) pulled by coal-fired steam locomotives with a leisurely cruise down the Connecticut River aboard a three-deck Mississippi-style riverboat.

7 Route 100, VT
📍K2–K6
Perhaps New England's ultimate road for leaf-peeping, Route 100 passes natural wonders like Moss Glen Falls,

follows the Mad River through several scenic villages, then rises high into the Green Mountains.

8 Deerfield River Rafting, MA

📍 C2 🏢 Zoar Outdoor 🕐 Apr–Oct
🌐 zoaroutdoor.com ↗

The Deerfield River has some of the most exhilarating rapids and magnificent gorges in New England. Nothing compares to the rush of bankside colors viewed from a raft during foliage season.

9 Boston's Emerald Necklace

📍 V4–W4 🌐 emeraldnechlace.org
Boston is blessed with an almost continuous chain of parks stretching from skyscrapers in the downtown area to its leafy suburbia. This walking and cycling route commences at Boston Common. During fall, the parks witness an explosion of browns, reds, oranges, and yellows.

10 Mount Monadnock, NH

📍 L6 🏢 Off Rte 124, west of Jaffrey 🕐 Sunrise–sunset daily
🌐 nhstateparhs.org ↗

The 3,165-ft- (965-m-) high summit of Mount Monadnock offers incredible views, especially in the fall. The boulder scramble to the top is well worth the effort. Reservations recommended.

TOP 10 COVERED BRIDGES

1. Burkeville Bridge, 1870
📍 C2 🏢 Rte 116, Conway, MA
Howe truss bridge stretching across the South River.

2. Cornish-Windsor Bridge, 1866
📍 L5 🏢 Rte 12A, Plainfield, NH
Town lattice over Connecticut River between New Hampshire and Vermont.

3. Hemlock Bridge, 1857
📍 M4 🏢 Off Rte 302, Fryeburg, ME
Paddleford truss over the Saco River.

4. Artist's Covered Bridge, 1872
📍 N3 🏢 Off Rtes 2 & 26, Newry, ME
Paddleford truss, also called the Sunday River Bridge.

5. Bulls Bridge, 1842
📍 B4 🏢 Rte 7, Kent, CT
Town lattice and queenspost over the Housatonic River.

6. Albany Covered Bridge, 1858
📍 M4 🏢 Dugway Rd, Albany, NH
Paddleford truss on Swift River.

7. Ashuelot Bridge, 1864
📍 K6 🏢 South of Rte 119, Winchester, NH
Town lattice truss over Ashuelot River.

8. Warren Bridge, 1880
📍 K4 🏢 East of Rte 100, Warren, VT
Oblique queenspost on Mad River.

9. Paper Mill, Silk, and Henry Bridges, 1840–2000
📍 J6 🏢 South of Rte 67A, Bennington, VT
Three bridges on Waloomsac River.

10. Stark Bridge, 1862
📍 M3 🏢 North Rd, Stark, NH
Paddleford truss spanning the Upper Ammonoosuc River in the village.

Historic Stark Bridge

MOUNTAIN SKI AREAS

1 Sunday River, Newry, ME

M3 15 South Ridge Rd Mid-Nov–mid-Apr sundayriver.com

The most accessible of Maine's high-mountain skiing, Sunday River sprawls across eight interconnected peaks, with 139 diverse trails served by ski lifts (including four high-speed quads). Lights extend evening skiing on most weekends and holidays. Snowmaking on 95 percent of terrain guarantees a long season. Evenings are enlivened by the popular Shipyard Brew Haus microbrewery *(shipyard brewhaussundayriver.com)*. During the summer it's a popular golf resort.

2 Bretton Woods, NH

M3 99 Shi Area Rd Mid-Nov–Apr brettonwoods.com

This is the largest ski area in New Hampshire featuring 464 acres (188 ha) of skiing and snowboarding on 63 trails, 35 glades, and three terrain parks. Consistently ranked among the top ski resorts both in the US and worldwide, Bretton Woods also offers a number of ski-stay packages through its close alliance with the Omni Mount Washington Resort *(p151)*, providing access to one of the last grand hotels in the White Mountains.

White Mountain towering behind the Mount Washington Resort

3 Mount Mansfield, Stowe, VT

K3 5781 Mountain Rd Mid-Nov–mid-Apr stowe.com

As the tallest of the attractive Green Mountains, Mount Mansfield challenges hikers every summer and fall. The area also attracts golfers to its impressive courses in the summer. Come winter, the Stowe Mountain Resort takes over the slopes with 116 trails and more mile-long lifts than any other resort in the East. With average annual snowfall of 333 inches (8 m), Stowe has a long season of deep snow.

4 Cannon Mountain, Franconia, NH

L3 260 Tramway Dr, Franconia Nov–mid-Apr cannonmt.com

One of the oldest ski areas in the US, Cannon has a refreshingly non-commercial feel about it, not to mention the spectacular White Mountains vistas from its 97 trails.

5 Killington, VT

K5 4763 Killington Rd Mid-Nov–mid-May killington.com

Killington Resort stretches across six mountain areas in central Vermont, providing 213 ski trails. As New England's largest ski resort, it also features 28 lifts, including three express gondolas and five express chairs, that give access to the highest

Skiers and boarders
at the Killington Resort

lift-served ski terrain in the state of Vermont. Snowboarders' needs are also catered for with The Stash and Dream Maker terrain parks as well as the 500-ft (152-m) Superpipe with 22-ft (7-m) walls.

6 Attitash, Bartlett, NH

📍M4 🚗Rte 302 🕐Dec–Apr
🌐attitash.com 🔗

Not as big or challenging as some New England areas, Attitash (and the nearby Bear Peak) have vistas of the White Mountains to make the skiing memorable. The longest vertical drop is 1,750 ft (534 m), and 8 lifts serve 76 trails.

7 Sugarloaf, Carrabasset Valley, ME

📍N2 🚗5092 Sugarloaf Access Rd
🕐Mid-Nov–late Apr 🌐sugarloaf.com 🔗

Offering the only lift-served skiing above the treeline in the east, this favorite resort features 54 miles (87 km) of trails crisscrossing Sugarloaf, Maine's second-highest peak at 4,237-ft (1,291-m). The continuous vertical drop of 2,820 ft (860 m) is New England's longest. The area particularly attracts experienced skiiers as sixty of Sugarloaf's 162 trails are rated difficult (black diamond) or expert (double black diamond).

8 Smugglers' Notch, Jeffersonville, VT

📍K3 🚗4323 Rte 108 S 🕐Mid-Nov–mid-Apr 🌐smuggs.com 🔗

Smugglers' Notch, an all-season family resort, is well known for its learn-to-ski programs and activities for kids. The resort stretches across three peaks, with 8 lifts serving 78 trails. The skiing at Smugglers' can be challenging, despite its family orientation; the Black Hole is the only triple black diamond trail in the Eastern US. Visit during the summer to enjoy other attractions that are offered such as fishing, water parks, canoeing, and golf.

9 Mad River Glen, Waitsfield, VT

📍K3 🕐Mid-Dec–early Apr
🌐madriverglen.com 🔗

This mountain, home to some of the East's most challenging skiing terrain, is run by a co-op of hardcore skiers who keep it simple: no snowboards, three double lifts that limit numbers on the slopes, and no fancy lodges or hotels with hot tubs.

10 Stratton Mountain, Stratton, VT

📍K6 🚗5 Village Lodge Rd
🕐Nov–Apr 🌐stratton.com 🔗

A pioneer in snowboarding, this resort is located in the Green Mountain National Forest near Manchester, a town popular with both skiers and shoppers. The 11 lifts serving 99 trails and top-ranked terrain parks include four six-person chair lifts. It's a great spot for golfing in the summer months.

OUTDOOR ACTIVITIES

1 Hiking
Two long-distance hiking trails cross New England, namely the Appalachian Trail (*p35*) and the Long Trail. The Appalachian Trail begins in Georgia and crosses Vermont and New Hampshire before ending in Maine, while the Long Trail traverses Vermont from south to north. Keen hikers can opt to join the Appalachian Mountain Club (*outdoors. org*) or the Green Mountain Club (*greenmountainclub.org*) for their exciting range of tour-led hikes.

2 Cross-Country Skiing
The epicenter of cross-country skiing is north-central Vermont, notably in Stowe, where the von Trapp family (of *Sound of Music* fame) introduced Nordic skiing. The von Trapp Family Lodge & Resort (*trappfamily.com*) now operates the largest cross-country ski center in the US. Another prime location is the Craftsbury Nordic Center (*craftsbury.com*), famous for its legendary cross-country ski races, which also offers day passes.

3 Schooner Sails
Seals, porpoises, and whales are your neighbors as you sail where the winds take you with the schooners of Maine's windjammer fleet. Visitors can select from a variety of sailing trips, ranging from a day-trip to week-long sojourns and more at the Maine Windjammer Association (*mainewindjammerfleet.com*).

4 Bird-Watching
Observe a variety of shore birds along with warblers and other migratory species at Wellfleet Bay Wildlife Sanctuary (*massaudobon.org*) on Cape Cod. The Audubon Society (*audubon. org/greenwich*) in Greenwich is home to seven sanctuaries and offers excellent bird-watching tours that attract many enthusiasts.

5 Surfing
The region of New England has plenty of coastline and is dotted with numerous surf-friendly beaches. The most notable can be found in Newport and Cape Cod: hire boards or take lessons at Rhody Surf (*rhodysurf.com*) or Sugar Surf (*sugarsurfcapecod.com*).

6 Fishing
Orvis (*orvis.com*) runs fly-fishing courses in Manchester in the state of Vermont. Novice fishers are taught about fly-fishing techniques and fishing gear. Frances Fleet (*francesfleet. com*), operating out of Galilee in Rhode Island, offers deep-sea trips along with whale-watching and dolphin tours.

7 Cycling
In Massachusetts, Minuteman Rail Trail cuts from Cambridge through Lexington and Concord. East Bay Bike Path is a tour of Narragansett Bay from Providence, Rhode Island. The Ashuelot Rail Trail from Keene to Hinsdale, New Hampshire, is a great way to explore

Hikers enjoying New England's fall colors

covered bridges (p63). TrailLink (trail link.com) connects bikers to numerous such trails in the New England area.

8 Whale-Watching

Large pods of whales summer on Stellwagen Bank. Take a cruise from Gloucester or Provincetown to look for finback, minke, and humpback whales, as well as dolphins. 7 Seas Whale Watch (7seaswhalewatch.com) offers daily narrated tours.

9 Kayaking and Canoeing

Explore Nauset Marsh by paddling among wading birds, or venture into the pristine waterways of Maine's Allagash Wilderness. For kayak rentals in Cape Cod, the Goose Hummock Shops (goosehummockshops.com) is the largest company, offering all manner of gear, from tandem to pedal-drive kayaks, for day or longer rentals. The Mahoosuc Guide Service (mahoosuc.com) provides guided canoe trips on the Allagash River.

10 White-Water Rafting

White-water rafting is hugely popular in Maine. Many trips depart from The Forks, a hamlet on the Kennebec. The Raft Maine Association (raftmaine.com) offers exciting and secure rafting excursions for outdoor enthusiasts of all ages on the Upper Kennebec River, the Penobscot River, and the lower Dead River.

White-water rafting in New England

TOP 10 NEW ENGLAND TRAILS

1. Walden Pond Path
Follow in the footsteps of Henry David Thoreau on this simple trail to an iconic pond. It's an easy hike, suitable for families.

2. Gulf Hagas
Often known as the "Grand Canyon of Maine," this gorge offers spectacular vistas and is a popular hiking destination along the state's section of the Appalachian Trail.

3. Tumbledown Mountain
This challenging loop offers scenic lakeside and mountain views in western Maine. Some take the less strenuous route to the top via the Brook Trail or the Park Ridge Trail.

4. Arethusa Falls Trail
This short New Hampshire trail ends with stellar views of one of the state's tallest waterfalls, Arethusa Falls.

5. Mount Major
Expect gorgeous views of Lake Winnipesaukee on this moderately challenging trek, which is marked with blue dashes.

6. Welch-Dickey Loop Trail
A popular 4-mile (6-km) White Mountains trail near Thornton, the Welch-Dickey Loop showcases the classic beauty of New Hampshire's mountains.

7. Great Blue Hill via Skyline Trail
Located in the Blue Hills Reservation, this trail is often considered the best hiking opportunity near Boston. You can see the skyline on a clear day.

8. Lye Brook Falls Trail
Spot one of the state's tallest waterfalls on this scenic trail through southwestern Vermont.

9. Stowe Pinnacle Trail
A steep and rocky route, this trail offers gorgeous views of Stowe's surrounding mountains.

10. Sleeping Giant Tower Trail
This central Connecticut trail promises scenic forest views and a four-story stone observation tower at the top.

SPECTATOR SPORTS

1 Baseball
New England's passion for baseball goes way back. The state's most famous team, the Boston Red Sox, was founded in Massachusetts in 1901, and they've been playing in their home ground of Fenway Park *(p23)* since 1912. This is the oldest active ballpark in Major League Baseball, and it remains a must-visit for fans of the sport. Not venturing to Boston? Catch the Worcester Red Sox in Massachusetts or the Portland Sea Dogs in Maine instead.

2 NFL
Football fans flock to Gillette Stadium, the base of six-time Superbowl champions, the New England Patriots *(patriots.com)*, but there's plenty more beyond the NFL. Semi-pro teams abound across the region – catch the Rhode Island Riptide or the Middleboro Cobras – or join fans cheering on the college football teams of universities such as Boston College and the University of Connecticut.

3 Basketball
New England isn't just the home of basketball legends, it's also the place where the sport was invented. Physical

WNBA team, the Connecticut Sun, at the Mohegan Sun Arena

education teacher James Naismith came up with the rules of the game in 1891, in Springfield, Massachusetts – the city now hosts the Naismith Memorial Basketball Hall of Fame *(p71)* – and the rest, as they say, is history. Today, the region's biggest teams are the Boston Celtics *(nba.com)*, who play at TD Garden, and the WNBA team, the Connecticut Sun *(sun.wnba.com)*, who shoot hoops at Mohegan Sun Arena.

4 Ice Hockey
Hockey is deeply rooted in New England culture, with the NHL's Boston Bruins *(nhl.com)* earning six Stanley Cup championship trophies since their introduction in 1924. College hockey is popular as well, thanks to the Boston Beanpot, a famed tradition that pits four esteemed Massachusetts universities (Harvard, Northeastern, Boston College, and Boston University) against each other for the championship trophy.

5 Rowing
Given the region's lengthy coastline, it's no surprise that watersports are a hit in New England. Numerous events take place throughout the year, but one in particular stands out. Since its debut in 1965, Boston's Head of the Charles Regatta *(hocr.org)* has become a worldwide phenomenon, drawing in more than 300,000 spectators and participants every year in October.

6 Running
The world's oldest annual marathon, the Boston Marathon *(baa.org)* has tested both elite and amateur runners since it began in 1897. Its iconic status means that beyond being simply tough to race, it's also tough to get into. If you don't get a spot, consider an alternative in the region: the Vermont City Marathon and Cape Cod's Falmouth Road Race promise gorgeous scenery and plenty of challenging terrain.

New England Revolution playing at Gillette Stadium

7 Soccer

While it's often overshadowed by the "Big Four" sports of the US (MLB, the NBA, the NFL, and the NHL), soccer does have its share of dedicated fans across New England. Check out small-scale clubs like Rhode Island FC, who are making a name for themselves in the region, and Major League Soccer teams such as the New England Revolution, who play at Gillette Stadium.

8 Motorsports

New Hampshire is an auto-racing fan's paradise, hosting major NASCAR and IndyCar events each year at the New Hampshire Motor Speedway (nhms.com), a course that's also known as "The Magic Mile". Further south, the New England Dragway (nedragway.com) is another popular attraction for (you guessed it) drag racing.

9 Toboggan

New England's icy winters offer prime conditions for the US National Toboggan Championships, a February festival that's held each year in Maine. While this event has drawn spectators for years, the region also offers plenty of opportunities for solo tobogganing.

10 Golf

Golf has a long history in New England, with the Newport Country Club hosting the first US Open back in 1895. Since then, the region has hosted a variety of other tournaments, including the Massachusetts Amateur and the New England Amateur.

TOP 10
SPORTS ICONS

1. Tom Brady
Famed New England Patriots quarterback who earned six Super Bowl rings with the team.

2. Jenny Thompson
New Hampshire swimmer who claimed eight Olympic golds from 1992 to 2004.

3. Ted Williams
Famed Red Sox hitter with the highest on-base percentage in MLB history.

4. Bobby Orr
Ice hockey icon best known for his exemplary defense skills for the Boston Bruins.

5. David "Big Papi" Ortiz
Red Sox hero who was instrumental in winning the 2004 World Series.

6. Patrice Bergeron
Longtime Boston Bruins center who spent 19 seasons with the team.

7. Joan Benoit
Maine native who won the first women's Olympic marathon in 1984.

8. Bill Russell
Celtics center with 11 NBA championships and a prominent legacy in the civil rights movement.

9. Aly Raisman
Massachusetts local who served as captain of the winning 2012 and 2016 US women's Olympic gymnastics teams.

10. Larry Bird
Boston Celtics legend who won multiple awards and is considered one of the greatest shooters in NBA history.

Basketball legend Larry Bird

FAMILY ATTRACTIONS

1 Ramblewild, Lanesborough, MA
📍 B2 🏠 110 Brodie Mountain Rd
🕐 Apr–Oct: Wed–Sun (book in advance) 🌐 ramblewild.com ↗

An eco-adventure center, Ramblewild is the perfect place for thrill-seekers, with an aerial adventure park, a lodge and a picnic area. It is home to eight trails of varying difficulty that wind through the canopy, featuring logs, nets, ziplines, and rope bridges.

2 Boston Children's Museum
📍 X4 🏠 308 Congress St
🕐 9am–4pm Wed–Mon (first Sat of every month: from 10am) 🌐 bostonchildrensmuseum.org ↗

One of the best children's museums in the US, the Boston Children's Museum has interesting exhibits on science, health, and the arts. Hands-on learning fills two former wool warehouses. Kids can scale a climbing sculpture, explore the magic of soap bubbles, or join in shows on KidStage.

3 Dinosaur State Park, Rocky Hill, CT
📍 C4 🏠 400 West St 📞 860 529 5816
🕐 9am–4:30pm Tue–Sun ↗

More than 500 dinosaur fossil tracks, preserved beneath a geodesic dome, captivate children at one of North America's largest track sites. Life-size dioramas re-create scenes from the Jurassic and Triassic eras.

4 McAuliffe-Shepard Discovery Center, Concord, NH
📍 M5 🏠 2 Institute Dr 🕐 Mid-Jun–late-Aug: 10:30am–4pm daily 🌐 starhop.com ↗

Named after astronauts Alan B. Shepard and Christa McAuliffe, this space-exploration center features a 10K projection system. With its many spacecrafts and simulators on display, it's the perfect place for budding astronomers and science enthusiasts.

5 Six Flags New England, Agawam, MA
📍 C3 🏠 Rte 159 🕐 Hours vary, check website 🌐 sixflags.com ↗

Some of the fastest, tallest, wildest, and most gut-wrenching thrill rides in the country await at this Six Flags amusement park located beside the Connecticut River.

6 Roger Williams Park and Zoo, Providence, RI
📍 E4 🏠 1000 Elmwood Ave
🕐 Hours vary, check website 🌐 rwpconservancy.org ↗

Visitors can ride the carousel or enjoy a boat ride on the lake in this sprawling park, and visit the Museum of Natural History, described as "the people's university," the planetarium, and the Botanical Center. More than 100 species roam naturalistic settings in themed areas of the zoo.

Exhibit at the Dinosaur State Park

Ben and Jerry's Ice Cream Factory in Vermont

7 Ben and Jerry's Ice Cream Factory, Waterbury, VT

The factory tour of Ben and Jerry's (p117) is a real hoot. The goal is the tasting room at the end, where you might sample flavors in development.

8 Basketball Hall of Fame, Springfield, MA

C3 1000 Hall of Fame Ave 10am–5pm daily hoop hall.com

This complex in the birthplace of basketball celebrates the sport with footage of games, star players' memorabilia, and interactive exhibits that are suitable for kids. Around 200,000 basketball fans visit its Hall of Fame Museum each year.

9 Lake Compounce, Bristol, CT

C4 185 Enterprise Dr Hours vary, chech website lahecomp ounce.com

A 1911 carousel, a 1927 roller coaster, and an antique trolley maintain the ambience of this amusement park. Most attractions, shows and restaurants are wheelchair accessible.

10 New England Aquarium, Boston

X3 Central Wharf 9am–5pm Mon–Fri, 9am–6pm Sat & Sun neaq.org

This aquarium has themed sections where children can view marine creatures and their habitats, and also learn about ocean conservation.

TOP 10
CAROUSELS

1. Bushnell Park Carousel
C4 Bushnell Park, Hartford, CT
A beautifully restored three-row hand-carved wooden carousel dating from 1914.

2. Heritage Museums & Gardens
G4 67 Grove St, Sandwich, MA
Located inside the American Art & Carousel Gallery, this carousel was hand-carved by Charles I. D. Looff Company in 1908.

3. Shelburne Museum
A vintage 1920s carousel that operates right outside the Shelburne Museum's Circus Building (p49).

4. Crescent Park Carousel
F4 700 Bullocks Point Ave, East Providence, RI
This Charles I. D. Looff showcase dates from 1895.

5. Flying Horse Carousel
E5 Bay St, Watch Hill, RI
This beachfront carousel is one of the oldest in New England.

6. Flying Horses Carousel
G5 Oak Bluffs Ave, Oak Bluffs, Martha's Vineyard, MA
An 1876–8 C. W. F. Dare Company model, originally on Coney Island, NY.

7. Greenway Carousel
X3 191 Atlantic Ave, Boston, MA
Carousel with hand-carved figures of local animals including a lobster.

8. Story Land
M4 Rte 16, Glen, NH
A strikingly unusual early 20th-century German carousel.

9. Heritage State Park
C3 221 Appleton St, Holyoke, MA
This 1929 carousel has 20 standing horses and 28 jumpers.

10. Lighthouse Point Park
C5 2 Lighthouse Point Rd, New Haven, CT
A 1916 carousel with 72 original, hand-carved figures.

NEW ENGLAND FOODS

**Bottles of maple syrup
on sale in New Hampshire**

1 Maple Syrup
New Englanders take great pleasure in pouring on the maple syrup over a stack of pancakes or waffles. In late winter, you might encounter sugar houses in the north of New England boiling down the sap of sugar maple trees. Stop for a jug – you'll never find it cheaper.

2 Scallops
Scallops were popular in New England cooking long before they became a mainstay of gourmet restaurants. Look for them sautéed in butter, breaded and deep-fried, or tossed with linguine, herbs, and olive oil. Scallops are on almost every menu, not least because New Bedford, Massachusetts, lands more scallops than any other port in the world.

3 Cranberries
Popular in juices and muffins, cranberries are best known for the sugary sauce served as part of traditional Thanksgiving dinner. Massachusetts produces about a quarter of America's cranberry crop.

4 Lobster
One of the joys of a New England summer is setting a steamed lobster on a picnic table, cracking it with a rock, and savoring the sweet meat with melted butter. *Homarus americanus*, often called "Maine lobster," is the world's largest crustacean, and is generally served at weights of 1¼–3 lb (0.5–1.3 kg). Another New England classic is the lobster roll, which features chilled lobster salad in a bun.

5 Clams
It's easy to get confused by New England clams. "Quahog" is the Indigenous name for the hard-shelled clam *Mercenaria mercenaria*, but the bivalve has other aliases. Small ones, known as "littlenecks," are served as the ever-popular battered-and-fried clam. Medium-sized quahogs are known as "cherrystones," and are often eaten raw. Big clams are stuffed and baked.

6 Oysters
New England's raw bars frequently serve oysters, which are found on sandy bottoms along the coast. Those cultivated in beds near Damariscotta Maine; Wellfleet, Massachusetts; and Norwalk, Connecticut are especially celebrated for their delicate, distinctive flavors.

**Oysters at a New
England raw bar**

Apple-picking at an orchard in New England

7 Heirloom Apples

Look for orchard farmstands selling apples in the fall. Many historic apple varieties can be traced to their New England birthplace by their names such as Roxbury Russet and Westfield-Seek-No-Further. Preservation efforts begun in the 1980s have borne fruit in the widespread availability of dozens of historic varieties.

8 Cheese

New England is home to some world-class farmstead cheeses. Small dairies make everything from fresh goat's milk chevre to aged, pungent blues. Somewhat larger Vermont cheese companies also produce superb American cheddar and Colby cheeses.

9 Blueberries

Whether you prefer the light blueberry accent of a muffin or the supreme intensity of a blueberry pie, there's no substitute for the tiny "wild" lowbush blueberry. Most wild blueberries are harvested in Maine from late July through August, but they freeze well, so blueberry baked treats are available all year.

10 Stone-ground Cornmeal

Order a "jonnycake" – a sweet cornmeal pancake – at any Rhode Island diner, and you'll be enjoying a culinary tradition going back to the region's first European colonists and the Indigenous people before them.

TOP 10 DRINKS

1. Green Mountain Coffee
Made in Waterbury, Vermont, this gourmet coffee roaster's blends are sold throughout the region.

2. Fresh Apple Cider
A New England tradition, apple cider is celebrated not only for its flavor but also for its health benefits. This freshly pressed and unfiltered apple juice is widely available in the fall.

3. Sam Adams Lager
The flagship brew of the Boston Beer Company, Sam Adams Lager launched the national craft beer revolution. This German-style lager offers a subtle hint of caramel.

4. Del's Lemonade
A thirst-quenching Rhode Island favorite, this iced drink contains only lemon juice, sugar, and shaved ice and is meant to be sipped without a straw, just like a true Rhode Islander.

5. Craft Brewed Cider
With the popularity of craft beers, small producers are now making many alcoholic craft ciders.

6. Coffee Milk
Rhode Island's official state drink is created by stirring coffee syrup into milk.

7. Sparkling Wines from Westport Rivers Winery
Estate-grown chardonnay and pinot noir grapes are used to make New England's best bubbly.

8. Moxie
Invented in 1876 by medical doctor Augustin Thompson, this soft drink with an appropriately medicinal aftertaste is now the official beverage of the state of Maine.

9. Lincoln Peak Vineyard Marquette
The signature red grape of this Vermont winery is a testament to artful winemaking, even in a harsh climate.

10. Frappe
Pronounced "frap," this thick milkshake includes ice cream and syrup in true New England style.

SHOPPING DESTINATIONS

1 League of New Hampshire Craftsmen Fair, NH

📍 L5 🏠 Mount Sunapee Resort, Newbury 🕐 Early Aug
🌐 nhcrafts.org ↗

Established in 1933, the League of New Hampshire Craftsmen Fair is the oldest craft fair in the US. More than 200 juried members and guest artists of the League offer their work, including jewelry, fine furniture, pottery, glass blowing, and weaving.

2 Woodbury, CT

📍 B5 🌐 antiqueswoodbury.com

Dealers in fine American and British antiques set up shop here around half a century ago. Since then, the town has become a go-to for folks seeking homey antiques and old-fashioned interior decorations.

3 Brimfield, MA

📍 D3 🏠 35 Palmer Rd
🕐 May, Jul & Sep 🌐 brimfield antiquefleamarket.com

Whether you're seeking Art Deco jewelry or vintage furniture, Brimfield is the place to visit. Antiques hunters from across the US and around the world converge on this small town for its three antiques shows held every year.

4 Shoppes at Buckland Hills, Manchester, CT

📍 C4 🏠 194 Buckland Hills Dr
🕐 10am–8pm Mon–Thu, 10am–9pm Fri & Sat, 11am–6pm Sun
🌐 theshoppesatbucklandhills.com

Central Connecticut's largest shopping area, the Shoppes at Buckland Hills features virtually every big-box national chain store, including discount electronics, decor, and home goods dealers like Yankee Candle.

5 Providence Place, Providence, RI

📍 E4 🏠 One Providence Pl 🕐 11am–8pm Mon–Thu, 10am–9pm Fri & Sat, 11am–6pm Sun 🌐 providence place.com

This mega-mall in downtown Providence has captured most of the retail activity in Rhode Island's capital. Stores occupy three levels, with entertainment and a food court.

6 Manchester, VT

📍 K6

Two dozen high-fashion shops entice fans of upscale bargains to Manchester Designer Outlets (manchesterdesigner outlets.com). The town also has outdoor outfitters such as Orvis (orvis.com) and Eddie Bauer (eddiebauer.com).

7 Freeport, ME

📍 P4 🌐 visitfreeport.com

Outdoors outfitter L. L. Bean (llbean.com) set the tone here when it opened in 1911. Freeport has since blossomed as a popular shoppers' paradise; more than 100 shops offer the biggest and best name brands, in American merchandising – often at substantial discounts.

Items on sale at Brimfield Antique Fair, Massachusetts

Well-stocked bookstore at
Harvard Square in Cambridge

8 Harvard Square, Cambridge, MA

F2 harvardsquare.com

America's most literary city is home to two comprehensive bookstores, both of which often host readings and signings. Also around Harvard Square are specialists in used books, poetry, and comic books.

9 Weston, VT

K5

General stores face each other across the main street in this picturesque village. The warren of rooms in the Vermont Country Store (*p117*) contains all kinds of clever gadgets, outdoors apparel, cooking utensils, and an excellent selection of foods from the New England area.

10 Wellfleet Flea Market, Wellfleet, MA

H4 Rte 6 Jun–Sep wellfleet cinemas.com/flea-market

Around 150 vendors gather at a drive-in theater near the end of Cape Cod, to sell an assortment of wares, including the occasional antique. Shoppers can browse the stalls for clothing, jewelry, and household goods, all available at a bargain. Remember to carry cash, as credit cards are not accepted.

TOP 10
SOUVENIRS

1. Maine Tourmaline Jewelry
The most famous Western Maine tourmalines are "watermelon" stones with pink centers and green edges.

2. Iconic Patriots Sweatshirt
Famed coach Bill Belichick is rarely seen in anything but the hooded gray New England Patriots sweatshirt.

3. Black Dog T-shirt
A black labrador T-shirt says "Martha's Vineyard" to anyone who has ever visited the Black Dog tavern there.

4. Vermont Snow Globe
Capture winter permanently by setting a snow globe on your shelf.

5. Lobster Keychain
The bright crimson of New England's quintessential crustacean makes your keys easier to spot.

6. Pine-Scented Pillow
Mainers have been selling these fragrant headrests since steamships first started running in the 1830s.

7. "This Car Climbed Mount Washington" Bumper Sticker
People will regard your old clunker with new respect.

8. Nantucket Lightship Basket
True folk art commands high prices for basket-purses with fashion cachet.

9. Woody Jackson "Holy Cow" Art
Jackson's cow-themed artwork, with the iconic black-and-white Vermont cows, is available on prints, cards, calendars, collectibles, and T-shirts.

10. Red Sox Baseball Cap
Show your loyalty in the epic rivalry between the Boston Red Sox and the New York Yankees.

Boston Red Sox baseball cap

NIGHTS OUT

1 Craft Breweries
Hardcore brewing buffs know that New England's craft-beer scene should never be overlooked. Aside from producing some iconic beers – like the Samuel Adams Boston Lager and Harpoon IPA – the region is home to some great small-scale breweries. Wet your whistle at beloved spots like The Alchemist Brewery *(p117)* in Vermont or New Park Brewing *(p109)* in Connecticut.

2 Theater Nights
New England's main hub for theater is undoubtedly Boston – this city has a thriving arts scene and a wealth of esteemed venues, including the Wang Theatre and Emerson Colonial Theatre. But there's singing and dancing beyond the capital, too. Further south, Rhode Island promises the grandiose Providence Performing Arts Center *(ppacri.org)*, while New Hampshire rewards those who venture north with the stunning Portsmouth Music Hall *(themusichall.org)*, an 1800s-era venue that hosts everything from musical performances to movie events.

3 Wine Bars
The cold New England climate isn't ideal for year-round grape-growing, but the region still offers a few gems for vinophiles. Plymouth visitors can try top-tier reds, whites, and rosés during a visit to Uva Wine Bar *(uvawine plymouth.com)*, while the region's Coastal Wine Trail *(coastalwinetrail.org)* shines a spotlight on the burgeoning prowess of southeastern New England, where wineries are scattered across Massachusetts and Rhode Island.

4 Live Music
The region that birthed the Cars, Aerosmith, and MGMT, New England has a rich music heritage. Live music isn't hard to find in major cities here, with spots like the Sinclair *(p88)* in Cambridge, Massachusetts acting as a beacon for indie acts, while neighboring Club Passim *(passim.org)* has hosted folk legends like Bob Dylan and Joni Mitchell. There's also Providence's Strand Ballroom for big-name acts *(thestrandri.com)* and New Hampshire's The Shaskeen *(p126)* for Irish music.

5 Classic Pubs and Taverns
Aside from great breweries, New England also has an array of old-school pubs and taverns. In Newport, the White Horse Tavern *(p101)* traces its heritage back to 1673, making it the oldest-operating bar in the nation. Meanwhile, in South Boston, L Street Tavern *(lsttavernsouthie.com)* is a go-to for homey charm and unfussy beer – it also starred in *Good Will Hunting*.

6 LGBTQ+ Nightlife
New England has long been a beacon for gay rights in the US and a safe space for the LGTBQ+ community. Provincetown *(p92)*, in Massachusetts,

The bright lights of Boston's theatre district

Rainbow flags lining the streets of Provincetown

is one of the liveliest hubs, with drag showcases, cabaret performances, and themed events occurring on the regular. Further west, Boston's South End neighborhood has traditionally served as the city's "gayborhood," while nearby Dorchester has emerged as another popular spot thanks to its abundance of queer spaces.

7 Rooftop Bars

Scenic New England has plenty of places for a drink with a view. In Maine, the aptly named The View (*16bayview. com*) overlooks Camden Harbor and slings up craft cocktails and tasty seafood, while the stylish Luna Rooftop Bar (*lunarooftopbarmaine.com*) promises more cocktails and great views of Portland. For an even better selection, head to Boston (*p88*).

8 Ghost Tours

Prefer your evenings with a side of spooky? New England has you covered. The dark legacy of Salem (*p87*) has given rise to paranormal tours across this Massachusetts city, while the state capital offers a chance to explore Boston's centuries-old resting grounds during a Ghosts and Graveyards trolley ride (*ghostsandgravestones.com*). Down in Rhode Island, Newport also joins in on the fun with the Olde Town Ghost Walk (*ghostsofnewport.com*), an eerie evening stroll past colonial mansions and cobblestone roads (some of which may be haunted…).

9 Comedy Clubs

Boston is the heart of New England's comedy scene, with staple Laugh Boston (*laughboston.com*) hosting acclaimed national acts. Rhode Island's Comedy Connection (*ricomedyconnection.com*) is also a big draw for local and regional talent.

10 Sunset Cruises

Float beyond the capital's shoreline with Boston Harbor Cruises (*boston-sailing.com*); take a twilight turn around Martha's Vineyard; or cruise across the waters of New Hampshire's Lake Winnipesaukee with Mount Washington Cruises (*cruisenh.com*): there's no better time to sail than sunset.

NEW ENGLAND FOR FREE

1 August Adventures

Admission to multiple museums and cultural attractions throughout Massachusetts is free during the month of August. Check the website (*highland street.org*) for institutions that take part.

2 National Park Service Walking Tours, MA

📍 W3 🏛 Faneuil Hall, 1 Faneuil Hall Sq, Boston; nps.gov/bost

Park rangers offer a variety of free walking tours of Boston National Historical Park. They range from segments of the Freedom Trail (*p25*) to the Black Heritage Trail (*p23*).

3 Boston Public Library Tours, MA

📍 U4 🏛 Copley Sq, Boston 🕐 9am–8pm Mon–Thu, 9am–5pm Fri & Sat, 11am–5pm Sun 🖥 bpl.org

Docents lead informative tours of the splendid art and architecture of the Boston Public Library.

4 Hiking Trails

New England has no shortage of scenic trails. The Green Mountains (*greenmountainclub.org*), in Vermont, are a popular hiking destination. Another favorite is Rhode Island's Cliffwalk (*cliffwalk.com*) that skirts the backyards of some of Newport's most dramatic Gilded Age mansions.

5 Project Puffin Visitor Center, ME

📍 Q3 🏛 311 Main St, Rockland 🕐 May: 10am–5pm Wed–Sun; Jun–Oct: 10am–5pm daily 🖥 seabird institute.audubon.org/project-puffin-visitor-center

At the Project Puffin Visitor Center tourists can learn about the ongoing seabird restoration programs on Maine's offshore islands and experience live video and audio feeds of puffin rookeries – one of the great bird conservation success stories in the area.

6 Hampton Beach Concerts and Fireworks, NH

📍 N6 🏛 115 Ocean Blvd, Hampton Beach 🕐 Jun–Aug 🖥 hamptonbeach.org

Every night throughout the summer, free concerts of various music genres are held on Hampton Beach, capped off each Wednesday with a display of fireworks at 9:30pm.

Stunning interior of the Boston Public Library

Indo-Pacific exhibits at the Yale University Art Gallery

7 Yale University Art Museums, New Haven, CT

The art museums at Yale, including the University Art Gallery and the Center for British Art, have superb treasures in landmark Louis B. Kahn buildings. The Yale University Art Gallery features more than 100,000 objects, while the Yale Center for British Art is the largest museum of its kind outside the UK.

8 Morse Farm, Vermont

📍 K3 🏠 1168 County Rd, Montpelier 🕐 Early Sep–late May: 10am–5pm daily; late May–early Sep: 10am–7pm daily 🌐 morse farm.com 🔗

Operating since 1966, this charming family-run maple-syrup farm offers a free tour of its grounds. Visitors are also treated to samples of its delicious maple syrup.

9 Arnold Arboretum, MA

📍 F3 🏠 125 Arborway, Boston 🌐 arboretum.harvard.edu

Established in 1872, this combined botanical research facility and public park features 281-acres (114-ha) of rolling landscape crisscrossed with walking trails. The scent of lilac fills the air in May, but it's the vibrant foliage of broadleaf trees in fall that really draws the crowds here.

10 WaterFire, Providence, RI

Barnaby Evans' installation features braziers floating near the Providence waterfront, creating a magical aura for concerts and citywide celebrations (p80). Check the website for the schedule of events.

TOP 10 BUDGET TIPS

1. The Red Sox farm-team games organized in Worcester cost much less than a game at Fenway *(milb. com/worcester)*.

2. Purchase discounted tickets to see live theater, music, dance, and comedy performances in Boston *(calendar.artsboston.org/categories/ bostix-deals)*.

3. Buy inexpensive and fresh lunches or picnic ingredients directly from local farmers' markets.

4. Many museums and hotels offer discounts to senior citizens or members of the American Automobile Association (AAA). Students from abroad should carry an International Student Identity Card (ISIC) to claim discounts.

5. Purchase fuel between Tuesday and Thursday to take advantage of the week's lowest prices.

6. The America the Beautiful Pass covers admission and fees at more than 2,000 federal recreation sites *(nps.gov/findapark/passes.htm)*.

7. Many museums offer free admission periods each week. Check their websites for specific details.

8. Inquire about special family rates at attractions and museums for the best value.

9. Lunch is more affordable than dinner at most of the top restaurants in New England.

10. Weekly MBTA (Massachusetts Bay Transport Authority) passes offer big savings on subway and bus fares in and around Boston.

Reusable card used on the MBTA

FESTIVALS AND EVENTS

1 Winter Carnival, Stowe, VT
Late Jan
In Stowe, plummeting temperatures and the first snowfall are celebrated with snow golf, snow volleyball, and ice-carving (*gostowe.com*).

2 Patriot's Day, Lexington and Concord, MA
Third Mon in Apr
This re-enactment of the opening salvos of the American Revolution (*nps.gov/mima*) starts before dawn in Lexington and continues on to nearby Concord.

3 WaterFire, Providence, RI
May–Nov
Nothing epitomizes the glory of the Providence waterfront as well as WaterFire (*waterfire.org*), an environmental sculpture by Barnaby Evans. Its 80 floating bonfires, on the city's three downtown rivers, make a magical setting for a host of summer arts events.

4 International Festival of Arts and Ideas, New Haven, CT
Mid-Jun
Every June, New Haven holds hundreds of events (*artidea.org*), the majority of them free, including opera on New Haven Green, hip-hop poets, dance, and readings by Nobel Laureate authors.

5 Windjammer Days, Boothbay Harbor, ME
Late Jun
Seven days of family fun include windjammer cruise schooners (*windjammerdays.org*) and other tall ships in Boothbay Harbor, an antique boat parade, waterfront concerts, a craft fair, and fireworks.

6 Green River Festival, Greenfield, MA
Late Jun
Launching the summer festival season, the three-day Green River festival (*greenriverfestival.com*) in Greenfield features folk, bluegrass, Americana, indie rock, Cajun, and roots music in a fairground venue.

7 Independence Day Celebrations, Boston
Jul 4
The red-white-and-blue stripe marks the Fourth of July parade route in Bristol (*fourthofjulybristolri.com*), site of one of the most enthusiastic small-town parades in the US. The televised

**Enjoying the Newport Folk
Festival from the water**

Independence Day celebration in Boston is famous for its fireworks and Boston Pops concert (bso.org/pops).

8 Jazz and Folk Festivals, Newport, RI

Jul & Aug

For over 50 years, the Newport Jazz Festival (newportjazz.org) and the Newport Folk Festival (newportfolk.org) have been a focus for fresh talent as well as for star performers. Fort Adams State Park, set at the mouth of the harbor with views of Newport Bridge and the East Passage, serves as the venue.

9 Maine Lobster Festival, Rockland, ME

Late Jul–early Aug

More than 20,000-lb (9,000-kg) of lobster are steamed every year for this Rockland waterfront festival (maine lobsterfestival.com). Lobstermen race across floating crates, floats parade down the street, and a panel of judges selects a Lobster Festival Delegate to preside over the event.

10 Thanksgiving, Plymouth, MA

Fourth Thu in Nov

Two events mark Thanksgiving in Plymouth. The first is a re-enactment of the 1621 Thanksgiving, performed by locals, some of whom are descendants of *Mayflower* pilgrims. Another is the National Day of Mourning, an annual march held by the United American Indians of New England.

Float at the Maine Lobster Festival in Rockland

TOP 10 AGRICULTURAL FAIRS

1. Barnstable County Fair, MA
G5 ⦿ Mid-Jul
This Falmouth fair features a demolition derby and a moto-stunt show.

2. Cheshire Fair, NH
L6 ⦿ Jul–early Aug
This Swanzey fair features pony pulls, puppets, and country music.

3. Addison County Fair and Field Days, VT
J4 ⦿ Early Aug
Held in Vergennes, this is Vermont's largest agricultural fair, which showcases local products.

4. Brooklyn Fair, CT
D4 ⦿ Aug
This Brooklyn fair features Nashville entertainment, old-fashioned midway rides, and prize poultry displays.

5. Washington County Fair, RI
E5 ⦿ Mid–late Aug
Don't miss this fun rooster-crowing contest in Richmond.

6. Woodstock Fair, CT
D4 ⦿ Aug–early Sep
A long-established harvest celebration and rural homecoming event, this fair is held in Woodstock.

7. Champlain Valley Fair, VT
J3 ⦿ Aug–early Sep
Enjoy a range of events from extreme motorcycle shows to sheep and dairy exhibits in Essex Junction.

8. Eastern States Exposition, MA
C3 ⦿ Mid-Sep–Oct
New England's largest fair held in West Springfield features food, music, and livestock displays.

9. Fryeburg Fair, ME
M4 ⦿ Early Oct
A traditional agricultural fair in Fryeburg that also includes woodsmen competitions.

10. Topsfield Fair, MA
F2 ⦿ Oct
Originally a cattle fair in Topsfield, it now attracts farmers from across the country.

AREA BY AREA

Historical houses in Nantucket, Massachusetts

MASSACHUSETTS

All roads in New England lead to Boston. The region's capital is a busy metropolis, home to top universities, cutting-edge restaurants, and a wealth of history (much of which can be found along the Freedom Trail). There's no better place to start your New England adventure than here, but there's plenty more to see in Massachusetts, too. This scenic state is famed for its seaside, particularly the coastal peninsula of Cape Cod and its picture-perfect nearby islands (Martha's Vineyard and Nantucket) – all famed summer getaways. Inland, the leafy hills of the Berkshires beckon (particularly during the fall), while fascinating history awaits in towns such as Salem (notorious for its 17th-century witch trials) and Lowell (the heart of the region's industrial revolution).

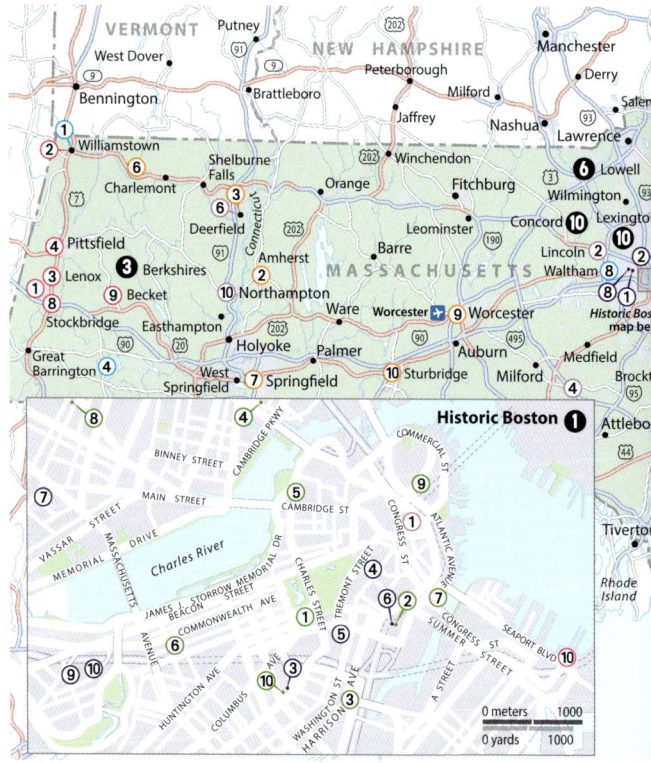

For places to stay in this area, see p148

1 Historic Boston

New England's largest city, Boston *(p22)* is nicknamed "the Hub," not just because it's the capital of the region, but because Bostonians think of their home as the center of all things historical, intellectual, and cultural in New England. Rightly so; Boston's history is inevitably the lead tale in New England's development and the city was at the heart of the American Revolution.

2 Martha's Vineyard

⧉ G5

The fish-shaped island of Martha's Vineyard covers 100 sq miles (259 sq km) and is only 7 miles (11 km) off the mainland. Up Island, its rustic western

Flower-decked porches at Martha's Vineyard

end, is a serene natural world that includes the sacred striped clay banks of Aquinnah. Down Island, its bustling eastern end, has the town of Vineyard Haven, the resort of Oak Bluffs, and the old whaling port of Edgartown.

3 Berkshires

Almost equidistant from Boston to the east and New York City to the south, the Berkshire Hills *(p28)* are a popular weekend getaway for city residents. The region's summer social schedule revolves around the performing arts, but the concentration of resident artists guarantees a rich off-season as well. The area is also perfect for hiking, mountain biking, and horseback riding.

4 New Bedford

⧉ F4

Settled in 1640, this deepwater port at the mouth of Buzzards Bay has always made its living from the sea. During the 1840s, pine-masted whaling barks would tie up at the wharves to offload whale oil from a three-year journey. By the mid-1800s, whaling profits had made it the richest port of its size in the world. Today the harbor creaks with great iron fishing boats that dredge Georges Bank for scallops, haul flounder from Nantucket Shoals, or venture offshore for cod.

Wampanoag exhibit at Pilgrim Hall Museum, Plymouth

5 Plymouth
☑ G3

In 1602, a group of Separatists, known as the English Pilgrims, crossed the Atlantic and sailed into Plymouth harbor to establish what is considered to be the first permanent English settlement in the Americas. The city is now steeped in history, with nearly every corner marked with a statue or a plaque. The Pilgrim Hall Museum *(pilgrim hall.org)* displays Pilgrim-era artifacts, with exhibitions on Wampanoag history and culture. Another attraction is the living history museum of Plimoth Patuxet *(p46)*, which depicts the settlement around 1627, and also contains exhibits devoted to Wampanoag life.

6 Lowell
☑ F2

Lowell was the first purpose-built city in the US, constructed in the 1820s as a factory town to manufacture textiles with equipment designs that were adapted from British mills. The textile industry is gone, but the canal network and looming mills remain as testament to the country's first tryst with the Industrial Revolution. After soaking up the mill history, visit Jack Kerouac Park, part of Lowell National Historical Park *(p47)*, to pay your respects to the Beat author who was born here.

7 Cape Cod

English explorer Bartholomew Gosnold literally put Cape Cod *(p26)* on the map in 1602 when he named the long curl of land for the fish so abundant in its waters. Cape Cod's soils are 15,000 years old – composed of sand and gravel that mark the southernmost advance of the last glacier – and it is hardly *terra firma*; every storm subtly reshapes the shore, making peninsulas into islands and vice versa. This transience of Cape Cod is part of its allure.

8 Nantucket
☑ H5

Off the coast of Cape Cod, Nantucket Island is a popular summer vacation spot. Unlike Martha's Vineyard, it is a small island, located 30 miles (48 km) offshore, making transportation costly. For this reason, only residents typically bring cars, though most, including tourists, prefer bicycles. Explore the venerable gray-shingled Nantucket town on foot, starting at the whaling museum *(p54)*. Then bike to Wauwinet to hike the dunes at Great Point, to

WITCH TRIALS

Salem exhibits mixed feelings about its witch history. On the 300th anniversary of the 1692 hysteria that led to the hanging of 19 "witches" and crushing of another, the city erected a memorial to the victims. But come Halloween, Salem is "witch city," capitalizing on its sensational past to draw curious visitors.

Siasconset to see rose-covered cottages, or Surfside to swim or fly kites on the beach.

9 Salem
☑ F2

In popular imagination, Salem is the city that tried and executed witches. But the 1692 trials are best seen as an aberration in the history of this vibrant city blessed with the art of the Peabody Essex Museum (p49) and a rich maritime history, recounted at the Salem Maritime National Historic Site (p55). In the 17th century, Salem's merchant princes were richer than the national treasury. Their grand houses still attest to their power.

10 Concord and Lexington
☑ E2 & F2

Lexington and neighboring Concord are forever linked in history as the settings for two bloody skirmishes that acted as catalysts for the American Revolution. On April 19, 1775, armed colonists called Minute Men clashed here with British troops on their way to Concord in search of rebel weaponry. A statue memorializing this struggle stands on Lexington Battle Green, where the battle is re-enacted every year in mid-April. Concord also gave the US its early literary voices in Ralph Waldo Emerson, Henry David Thoreau, and Louisa May Alcott. All three are buried at Concord's Sleepy Hollow Cemetery.

Colorful foliage during fall in Lowell

A DAY PEDALING FROM CAMBRIDGE TO CONCORD

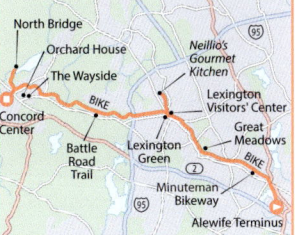

Morning

Start your journey through American history by taking the "T" to the **Alewife terminus** of the Red Line. From here, follow marked signs to the **Minuteman Bikeway** and pedal through Arlington, then watch for egrets, and herons along the edges of **Great Meadows** nature area. The bikeway passes the **Lexington Visitors' Center** of Minute Man National Historical Park (p46), perfect for a rest stop, and continues on to historic **Lexington Green**. Spot Daniel Chester French's *Minute Man* statue here, then cycle to **Neillio's Gourmet Kitchen** (No. 53) for a box lunch.

Afternoon

Just west of Lexington Green you switch from the Minuteman Bikeway to **Battle Road Trail**, an unpaved road that parallels the route of the running battle as British forces retreated in 1775; historical signposts explain the sights along the way. **North Bridge**, near another visitor center in the park, is especially evocative. At the end of the trail, visit **The Wayside** and **Orchard House** (p52) to learn about Concord's literary history. Lexington Road takes you into **Concord Center**, where you can return to Boston on the commuter rail.

Enjoying a live music show at House of Blues®

Bars and Nightlife in Boston

1. The Sinclair
 F2 52 Church St, Cambridge
 sinclaircambridge.com
Part gastropub and part music venue,
The Sinclair offers comfort fare and live
performances by indie bands.

2. Grace by Nia
 X4 60 Seaport Blvd
 gracebynia.com
Feast on southern classics like *gumbo*
while listening to jazz at this intimate
supper club – which also offers vegan
options. The cocktail lounge is a must.

3. Beehive
 V5 541 Tremont St
 beehiveboston.com
This bar-café hosts live jazz shows
by local artists. The creative bistro
menu is complemented by craft
beers and inventive cocktails.

4. Yvonne's
 W4 2 Winter Place
 yvonnesboston.com
This legendary dining spot exudes
old-school elegance with its opulent
interior, adding glamour to the
innovative and classic cocktails.

5. Nick's Comedy Stop
 V4 100 Warrenton St
 nickscomedystop.com
Renowned comedians from popular
TV shows headline at Nick's, Boston's
longest-running comedy club.

6. OFFSUIT
 W4 5 Utica St offsuitboston.com
This sleek speakeasy is one of the
coolest places for cocktails in Boston –
its espresso martinis are sublime.

7. Middle East
 S3 472–480 Massachusetts Ave,
Cambridge mideastclub.com
If you follow underground music,
you're probably already aware of
this legendary venue for new bands
that are looking to break through.

8. The Plough and the Stars
 W3 912 Massachusetts Ave,
Cambridge ploughandstars.com
Founded in 1969, this musical bar is
where Van Morrison penned part of his
Astral Weeks album. There is live music
from Thursday to Saturday.

9. Game On
 S5 82 Lansdowne St
 gameonboston.com
One of Boston's top sports bars,
Game On is built into the walls of
Fenway Park. With an entire wall
covered with flat-screen TVs there's
always, well, a game on.

10. House of Blues®
 S5 15 Lansdowne St
 houseofblues.com
This Boston-born chain offers
excellent Southern-inspired cuisine
and regular live-music performances.

Restaurants in Boston

PRICE CATEGORIES
For a three-course meal for one with
half a bottle of wine (or equivalent
meal), taxes and extra charges.

$ under $45 **$$** $45–$80 **$$$** over $80

1. Bistro du Midi
U4 272 Boylston St
bistrodumidi.com · $$$
Overlooking the Public Garden,
this elegant bistro serves fresh New
England produce with French flair.

2. Oya
W4 9 E St L daily & Sun–
Mon o-ya.restaurant · $$$
A modern Japanese restaurant, Oya
is celebrated for chef Tim Cushman's
inventive *sushi* and *omakase*.

3. Kaia
W5 370 Harrison Ave
kaiasouthend.com · $$$
Kaia's dishes are inspired by the vibrant
flavors of Greece. The *spanakopita*
(spinach and feta pie) is excellent.

4. Geppetto
U1 8100 N First St L the
lexingtoncx.com/geppetto · $$
Chef Will Gilson's Cambridge
restaurant serves Northern Italian
cuisine and specializes in pastas and
grilled meats.

5. Scampo, Liberty Hotel
V3 215 Charles St
scampoboston.com · $$$
Led by an award-winning chef, this
restaurant offers modern American
fare with a New England accent.

6. Little Whale
U4 314 Newbury St
littlewhaleboston.com · $$
This sleek spot offers a daily changing
selection of oysters, paying tribute
to New England marine catches.

7. Trade
X4 540 Atlantic Ave L, Sat,
Sun & Mon trade-boston.com · $$
Trade is the fine-dining anchor to
Greenway Park that links Downtown
and the waterfront. It is a hotspot for
Mediterranean-inspired bites, craft
beers, and designer cocktails.

8. Oleana
S2 134 Hampshire St, Cambridge
L oleanarestaurant.com · $$$
Expect eastern Mediterranean cuisines
at Oleana, with spicy dishes from
Turkey, Greece, and North Africa. Dine
at the outdoor tables in the garden.

9. Mare Oyster Bar
X3 3 Mechanic St L
mareoysterbar.com · $$$
Local oysters and crudo plates
complement Italian seafood dishes
in this sophisticated North End
restaurant. There's also a number
of delectable Italian desserts, as well
as a good selection of wines and
cocktails to pair with your meal.

10. Blackbird Doughnuts + Sally's Sandwiches
V5 492 Tremont St
blackbirddougnuts.com · $
This woman-led venture offers fresh,
delicious doughnuts, with new flavors
introduced monthly, alongside hearty
wraps, sandwiches, and coffee.

Oleana's leafy patio, in Cambridge, MA

The Best of the Rest

Lovely window display at a store in Rockport

1. Gloucester
📍 G2

Sticking 30 miles (42 km) out to sea on Cape Ann, Gloucester's harbor is a legendary fishing port and home to Rocky Neck Art Colony (p92).

2. Northampton and Amherst
📍 C3

Northampton and Amherst, both part of the Pioneer Valley region, are cities whose cultural life is centered around four colleges, including Smith, with its major art museum. Emily Dickinson Homestead, in Amherst, is a testament to the city's literary ties.

3. Deerfield
📍 C2

Situated alongside the Connecticut river, Deerfield is home to a mile-(1.5-km-) long central avenue, lined with clapboard homes. Around 60 of these remain within Historic Deerfield (historic-deerfield.org) and are carefully preserved. Some of the houses serve as museums, exhibiting a broad range of period furniture and decorative arts.

4. Ipswich and Essex
📍 F2 & G2

The sands of Crane Beach (p60) in Ipswich and the winding tidal river at Essex (p92) make these North Shore communities great for nature lovers. Both are famed for shellfish.

5. Rockport
📍 G2

The iconic Motif #1, a red fishing shed in the harbor, is among the most-painted subjects in this lovely village of art galleries and boutiques.

6. Mohawk Trail
📍 C2

This trail offers an ideal opportunity to experience the region's natural beauty. Follow Route 2 west from Greenfield over the Berkshire Mountains to North Adams to be wowed by foliage. Turnoffs lead to orchards, river rafting, mountain hiking, and sugar houses.

7. Springfield
📍 C3 🌐 springfieldmuseums.org

Founded in 1636, Springfield is known as the "city of firsts" as it is the birthplace of many creations such as the first American dictionary and the US's first gas-powered vehicle. Visitors can learn about its history at the Quadrangle, a group of cultural institutions that includes the Dr. Seuss Museum.

8. Newburyport
📍 N6

Its fantastic concentration of grand Federal-style homes makes Newburyport an essential stop for history buffs and preservationists. Birders flock to Plum Island at the harbor mouth for some of New England's best birding.

9. Worcester
📍 E3

Worcester has a top art museum (p48) and a unique indoor-outdoor museum, the EcoTarium (ecotarium.org).

10. Brimfield and Sturbridge
📍 D3

New England's rural heart bustles thrice a year with Brimfield antiques shows (p74). Old Sturbridge Village (p46) re-creates rural New England of 150 years ago.

Summer Performing Arts

1. Tanglewood
📍B3 🏠297 West St, Lenox
🕐Jun–early Sep Ⓦbso.org 🔗
Named for Nathaniel Hawthorne's
Tanglewood Tales, this world-renowned
music festival is held across the towns
of Stockbridge and Lenox. It's also the
Boston Symphony's summer home,
characterized by excellent musician-
ship and elaborate picnics.

2. Williamstown Theater Festival
📍B2 🏠1000 Main St, Williamstown
🕐Jul & Aug Ⓦwtfestival.org 🔗
Established in 1954 on the Williams
College campus, the Tony Award-
winning Williamstown Theater Festival
attracts film and TV directors who
come here to refine their stagecraft.
During the summer festival, celebrity-
spotting is popular here.

3. Shakespeare and Company
📍B3 🏠70 Kemble St, Lenox 🕐Late
May–mid Sep Ⓦshakespeare.org 🔗
Renowned for their Shakespeare
performances, this company also
develops and produces new plays
of social and political significance.

4. Barrington Stage Company
📍B2 🏠30 Union St, Pittsfield 🕐Mid-
Jun–Oct Ⓦbarringtonstageco.org 🔗
A wellspring of new plays and musicals,
Barrington Stage incubates electrifying
theater that often winds up playing
on Broadway. Notably, its musical, *The
25th Annual Putnam County Spelling
Bee*, has earned two Tony Awards.

5. Gloucester Stage Company
📍G2 🏠267 E. Main St, Gloucester
🕐Jun–Sep Ⓦgloucesterstage.com 🔗
Founded in 1979, this award-winning
theater company, next to Rocky Neck
Art Colony, stages socially relevant
dramas, comedies, and musicals.

6. Wellfleet Harbor Actors Theater
📍H4 🏠Rte 6, Wellfleet 🕐Jun–Oct
Ⓦwhat.org 🔗
Humor, passion, a sense of the
absurd, and a sharp political edge
are hallmarks of this small troupe.

7. Cape Playhouse
📍H4 🏠820 Rte 6A, Dennis 🕐Mid-
Jun–Sep Ⓦcapeplayhouse.com 🔗
America's oldest professional
summer theater puts on classics,
comedies, mysteries, and musicals.

8. Berkshire Theater Group
📍B3 🏠Main St, Stochbridge
🕐Mid-Jun–Dec Ⓦberkshire
theatregroup.org 🔗
The 1888 Stockbridge Casino and
Pittsfield's 1910 Colonial Theater
make grand settings for new, classic,
and contemporary theater.

9. Jacob's Pillow Dance Festival
📍B3 🏠358 George Carter Rd,
Bechet 🕐Mid-Jun–late Aug
Ⓦjacobspillow.org 🔗
Enjoy performances by leading US
and international dance companies
in a magical setting.

10. Leader Bank Pavilion
📍F2 🏠290 Northern Ave, Boston
🕐Jun–Sep Ⓦlivenation.com 🔗
This 5,000-seat harborside outdoor
pavilion has hosted performances by
legendary artists such as Frank Sinatra,
Diana Ross, and Stevie Wonder.

**Van Morrison with his band
at the Leader Bank Pavilion**

Places to Shop

1. Faneuil Hall Marketplace
📍 X3 🏠 Boston

Established in 1742, Faneuil Hall is a Boston landmark, serving as a waterfront marketplace and meeting hall. It consists of Quincy Market, along with the North and South Markets. Quincy Market has an excellent food court and over 40 vendors selling local wares. The North and South Markets feature a variety of boutiques and specialty shops.

Pushcarts selling wares at the Faneuil Hall Marketplace

2. deCordova Museum Store
📍 F2 🏠 51 Sandy Pond Rd, Lincoln

Modern art, mostly by New England artists, is the focus of deCordova Sculpture Park and Museum. The museum store sells a range of art supplies, jewelry, wearable art, and toys.

3. Fuller Craft Museum
📍 F3 🏠 455 Oak St, Brockton

This premier museum carries an extensive selection of artists' jewelry, which is displayed alongside work in glass, ceramic, fiber, and wood.

4. Wrentham Village Premium Outlets
📍 F3 🏠 1 Premium Outlets Blvd., Wrentham

Bargain-hunters from all over New England converge on this mall, where more than 150 stores are dedicated to designer apparel and an array of upscale housewares.

5. Sandwich Glass Museum
📍 G4 🏠 129 Main St, Sandwich

The museum shop carries excellent reproductions of historic pressed glass from Sandwich and blown glass from the museum's own on-site glassblowing studio.

Vase at Sandwich Glass Museum

6. Yankee Candle Village
📍 C2 🏠 Rtes 5 & 10, South Deerfield

The leading US producer of scented candles offers the world's largest candle selection, all-year Christmas shopping, and custom candle-making.

7. Rocky Neck Art Colony
📍 G2

It is not difficult to see why this rocky peninsula is such an inspiration for artists. You can walk from cottage to cottage to see (and buy) paintings created by resident painters in one of the oldest art colonies in America.

8. Essex
📍 G2

There are more than a dozen antiques shops in this community. Look out for nautical artifacts, porcelain, vintage furniture, and excellent oil paintings.

9. Provincetown
📍 H3

In summer, Friday is "gallery night" here. Galleries set out wine and cheese to attract prospective buyers.

10. Paradise City Arts Festivals
📍 C3 🏠 Rte 9 and Old Ferry Rd, Northampton

Held at the Three-County Fairgrounds in Northampton, this festival is a great opportunity to explore and buy local crafts by designers and artists.

Restaurants

1. Mezze Bistro + Bar
🅿 B2 🅰 777 Cold Spring Rd, Williamstown 🕒 L Mon & Tue 🌐 mezzerestaurant.com· $$$
Local growers provide the meat, produce, and cheeses for this highly adept American bistro.

2. Cape Sea Grille
🅿 H4 🅰 31 Sea St, Harwich Port 🕒 L, Mon & Tue 🌐 capeseagrille.com · $$$
Enjoy a candlelight dinner at this restaurant, offering delicious fish and vegetable dishes in an elegant setting.

3. Back Eddy
🅿 F4 🅰 1 Bridge Rd, Westport 🕒 L Mon–Fri, Jan–Mar 🌐 thebackeddy.com · $$
Casual cuisine and a raw bar serving Westport shellfish and wood-grilled local meats and fish. The outdoor bar has a convivial social scene.

4. Old Inn on the Green
🅿 B3 🅰 134 Hartsville–New Marlboro Rd 🕒 L, Mon & Tue 🌐 oldinn.com · $$$
Set in a 18th-century inn, this American bistro offers candlelit dining and a menu of fresh, innovative fare.

5. Topper's
🅿 H5 🅰 120 Wauwinet Rd, Nantucket 🕒 Late Oct–Apr 🌐 wauwinet.com/ dining/toppers · $$$
Savor Beef Wellington, skillet-roasted halibut, or buttered lobster in a truffle emulsion, all served in a scenic waterfront setting.

6. Sweet Life Café
🅿 G5 🅰 63 Circuit Ave, Oak Bluffs, Martha's Vineyard 🕒 Tue 🌐 sweetlifemv.com · $$$
At Sweet Life, enjoy a seasonal menu, featuring local vegetables and fish, paired with an extensive wine list.

PRICE CATEGORIES

For a three-course meal for one with half a bottle of wine (or equivalent meal), taxes and extra charges.

$ under $45 $$ $45–$80 $$$ over $80

7. Tonno
🅿 G2 🅰 2 Main St, Gloucester 🕒 L 🌐 tonnorestaurant.com · $$
Italian-style seafood tops the menu at this elegant fine dining restaurant. There's a vast variety of craft beer and wines, too.

8. Il Capriccio
🅿 F2 🅰 704 Main St, Waltham 🕒 L, Sun 🌐 ilcapricciowaltham.com · $$$
This charming restaurant offers a Northern Italian menu, which frequently changes depending on the harvest and catch of the day. It also has an extensive wine list.

9. Ledger
🅿 F2 🅰 125 Washington St, Salem 🕒 Brunch Sun, D Wed–Sun · $$$
Housed in an old bank, this upscale bistro serves New England cuisine made with the finest local ingredients.

10. Stars
🅿 H4 🅰 Chatham Bars Inn, 297 Shore Rd 🕒 Hours vary, check website 🌐 chathambarsinn.com/dining/stars · $$$
This four-star Cape Cod restaurant serves traditional steakhouse fare and excellent seafood. Don't forget to try the creative dessert menu.

Soft-shell steamed clams, a New England classic

RHODE ISLAND

Rhode Island is nicknamed the Ocean State for good reason. Most of America's smallest state – also known as "little Rhody" – lies along its 384-mile (618-km) coastline. Its scenic shores are primed for adventure, promising both bathing beaches with gentle waves and sweeping sandy stretches popular with surfers; you'll find America's top yachting harbor here, too. Its cities are equally enticing. Head to Newport to gaze upon majestic Gilded Age mansions, perched dramatically atop the cliffs. Or, spend a few days in the state's capital, Providence; this vibrant city is a national leader in design and fine arts, as well as a champion of chef-driven contemporary cuisine. Aside from the big sites, there are numerous low-key little towns, perfect for days away from the crowds and off-the-beaten-track adventures.

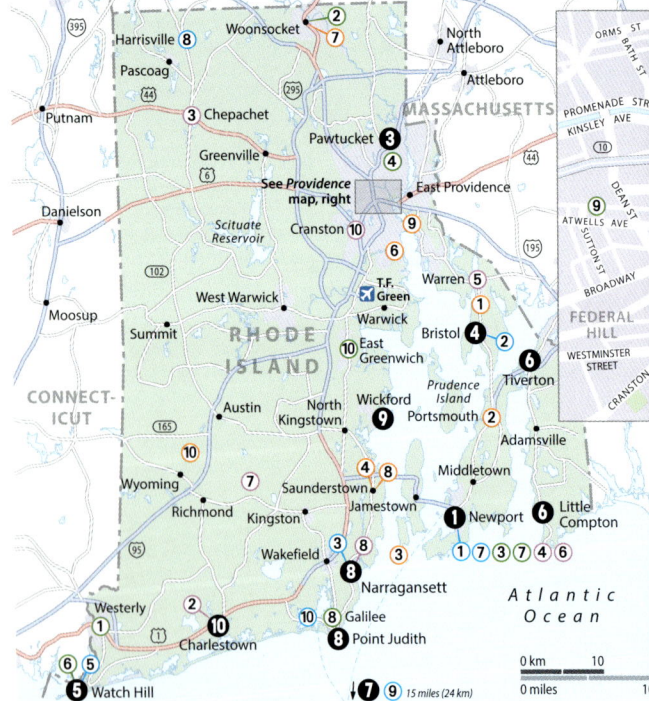

For places to stay in this area, see p149

Atwells Avenue in the Federal Hill District, Providence

1 Newport

Nineteenth-century mansions and a snug harbor dotted with racing yachts and speedboats make this city one of the best summer destinations in the region. The downtown area is a history buff's delight *(p42)*.

2 Providence
📍 E4

The Rhode Island School of Design (RISD) *(p51)*, a top US art and design school, provides the zing to downtown Providence, a city also known as a major food hub. The museums and historic houses of Benefit Street's "Mile of History" capture 250 years of New England life. Visit the traditionally Italian district of Federal Hill for restaurants, *salumerias*, and coffee shops.

3 Pawtucket
📍 E4

Due to its proximity to the Blackstone River, the city of Pawtucket flourished greatly in the past: Samuel Slater set up the country's first successful cotton mill *(p47)* here in 1793, jump-starting the American Industrial Revolution. Today the city is best known for the vast Rhode Island Antiques Mall, and its September Dragon Boat Race.

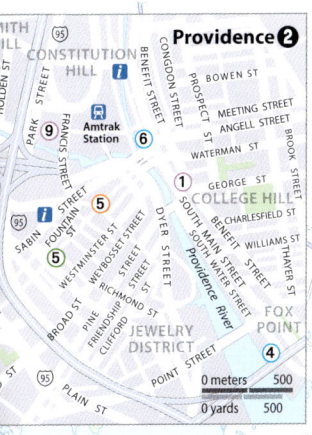

Participating in the annual Dragon Boat Race, Pawtucket

Biking alongside Narragansett Bay in Bristol

4 Bristol
📍 F4

Renowned for jubilant Independence Day celebrations (p81) that date from 1785, Bristol is a charming deep-water seaport on the eastern side of the Narragansett Bay. The village is home to the Herreshoff yacht-building firm, whose museum (herreshoff.org) traces the history of the America's Cup, the most prestigious prize in yacht-racing. Visit the Blithewold estate (blithewold.org), where Rhode Island couples flock to wed with spectacular vistas of the bay as a backdrop.

5 Watch Hill
📍 E5

The glorious beaches of South County, the Rhode Island shore west of Point Judith, reach their apogee at Watch Hill, an old-fashioned and affluent seaside community in the town of Westerly. The village also takes immense pride in its historic Flying Horse Carousel.

6 Tiverton and Little Compton
📍 F4 & F5

Occupying their own little peninsula between Narragansett Bay and the Massachusetts border, the towns of Tiverton and Little Compton are insulated from the modern world by woods and rolling farmlands. Watch for roadside stands selling seasonal strawberries and sweetcorn. Wine grapes also flourish: visit Carolyn's Sakonnet Vineyard (sakonnet wine.com) for tours and tastings.

7 Block Island
📍 E6

Just 15 miles (24 km) off the coast, Block Island has long been a summer vacation haven for New Englanders. Thirty miles (48 km) of nature trails crisscross the pear-shaped island, and a quarter of the land is protected against development. Crescent Beach, just north of the Victorian resort village of Old Harbor, has fabulous swimming and – when the wind is right – good surfing. Deep-sea fishing excursions are popular day-trips from Old Harbor.

8 Narragansett and Point Judith
📍 E5

In 1900, a fire destroyed the hotels and casino that made Narragansett Beach a high-society resort. Today, families and sunbathers rule the beach while surfers in wetsuits ride the waves. The peninsula going south ends at Point Judith, which shelters the fishing port of Galilee. Whale-watching and

CLAIBORNE PELL BRIDGE

Constructed in 1966–69, Newport's Claiborne Pell Bridge is the longest bridge in Rhode Island and the largest suspension bridge in New England. With a main span of 1,601 ft (488 m) and an overall length of 11,247 ft (3,428 m), the bridge arcs over Narragansett Bay to connect Jamestown and Newport.

deep-sea-fishing cruise vessels share berths with the fishing boats. Don't miss fish dinner at George's of Galilee *(p100)*.

9 Wickford
🔲 E5

Artists and craftspeople have long flocked to this historic, picturesque village near North Kingstown, and their galleries and stores are big lures for day-trippers. What few visitors realize is that the village's location on the west side of Narragansett Bay makes it the ideal launching point for exploring the bay by sea kayak. Inquire about expert guided paddles at the Kayak Centre *(kayakcentre.com)*.

10 Charlestown
🔲 E5

Named after British King Charles II, Charlestown enjoys a 4-mile (6.5-km) coastline, encompassing the largest saltwater marshes in the state. You'll find some of New England's best birding for wading birds and waterfowl in this watery ecosystem between land and sea. The sprawling Ninigret Park comprises a beachfront, tracks for cyclists and bladers as well as a swimming pool and tennis courts. Also part of the park is the Frosty Drew Nature Center and Observatory *(frosty drew.org)* where astronomy buffs congregate every clear Friday night to scan the skies. Another popular spot is Charlestown Breachway State Beach, a sweeping beach with views of Block Island, just off the coast.

Picturesque Charlestown Breachway State Beach

NAVIGATING FROM PROVIDENCE TO NEWPORT

Morning

Start the day in **Providence** *(p94)* with a stroll around **Waterplace Park**, a pool and amphitheater between Francis and Exchange streets. Cross the Steeple Street Bridge, noting the ionic columns of the **First Baptist Church in America** on the left. Then, pop into **Ellie's** *(250 Westminster St)* for a pastry and coffee before entering the **RISD Museum** *(p50)*, paying special attention to the modern art. The attached store specializes in creations by RISD-affiliated designers. Take the I-195 east to Rte 136 south to reach picturesque **Bristol** *(p97)*. Eat *stuffies* (stuffed clams) for lunch at **Thames Waterside Bar & Grill** *(251 Thames St)* and see the America's Cup exhibits at the **Herreshoff Marine Museum** *(1 Burnside St)* before continuing south on Rte 114 to **Newport** *(p94)*. Here, take a Gilded Age mansion tour of **The Breakers** *(44 Ochre Pt Ave)*, followed by a sunset cruise in Newport harbor aboard a schooner or yacht.

Evening

Make a night of it at **The Landing** *(30 Bowen's Wharf)*, a large waterfront eating and drinking establishment known for its raw bar, live music, and maritime-themed cocktails.

The Best of the Rest

1. Audubon Society of Rhode Island Nature Center and Aquarium

🄟 F5 🄐 1401 Hope St, Rte 114, Bristol 🄞 Hours vary, chech website 🅦 asri.org 🄸

Spread over 28 acres (11.3 ha), this natural history museum gives insight into Rhode Island's local habitat and wildlife through interactive displays.

2. Green Animals Topiary Garden

🄟 F5 🄐 380 Cory's Lane, off Rte 114, Portsmouth 🄞 Late May–early Oct: daily 🅦 newportmansions.org 🄸

A Rhode Island Red rooster is one of the 80 topiaries at the US's oldest topiary garden, located in Portsmouth.

3. Beavertail Lighthouse Museum

🄟 E5 🄐 Beavertail State Park, Jamestown 🄞 Hours vary, chech website 🅦 beavertaillight.org

Built in 1856, this lighthouse is located at the entrance of Narragansett Bay. The lighthouse keeper's house is now a museum.

4. Casey Farm

🄟 E5 🄐 2325 Boston Nech Rd, Saunderstown 🄒 401 295 1030 🄞 Mid-May–Oct: 8:30am–12:30pm Sat (Jun–mid-Oct: also 1–3pm Tue) 🄸

Get a glimpse of Rhode Island's agricultural past at the regional farmers' markets, held here on Saturdays.

5. The Providence Rink

🄟 E4 🄐 2 Kennedy Plaza, Providence 🄞 Hours vary, chech website 🅦 theprovidencerink.com 🄸

Skate in the shadow of the state's tallest skyscraper, the 428-ft (130-m) Art Deco "Superman Building," at this outdoor skating rink. It hosts a variety of events throughout the year.

6. Pawtuxet Village

🄟 E4 🄐 Warwich

Pawtuxet Village is known for "Gaspee Days" – a celebration commemorating the burning of British ship HMS *Gaspee* in 1772 and featuring parades, concerts, and spectacular fireworks.

7. Museum of Work and Culture

🄟 E3 🄐 42 S. Main St, Woonsochet 🄞 Sun & Mon 🅦 rihs.org 🄸

This former textile mill, now a museum, details the lives of those who worked in it and in other local factories.

8. Gilbert Stuart Birthplace and Museum

🄟 E5 🄐 815 Gilbert Stuart Rd, Saunderstown 🄞 Hours vary, chech website 🅦 gilbertstuartmuseum.org 🄸

Artist Gilbert Stuart painted the celebrities of his day. A tour of his birthplace explores his beginnings.

9. East Bay Bike Path

🄟 F4

Zip down this bayside path for views of the Narragansett Bay on one side, and herons and egrets on the other.

10. Tomaquag Museum

🄟 E5 🄐 390A Summit Rd, Exeter 🄞 10am–5pm Wed, 10am–2pm Sat 🅦 tomaquagmuseum.org 🄸

This center promotes understanding of Indigenous culture. An expanded new facility is in the works.

Colorful Gaspee Parade in Pawtuxet Village

Places to Shop

1. RISD Store
📍 E4 🏠 Chace Center, 30 N Main St, Providence 🕐 9am–5pm Mon–Fri, noon–5pm Sat & Sun 🌐 risdstore.com
Creativity abounds at the RISD Store which showcases fashion, furniture, toys, and tools from alumni and faculty members of the school.

2. The Fantastic Umbrella Factory
📍 E5 🏠 4820 Old Post Rd, Charlestown 🌐 fantastic umbrellafactory.com
No umbrellas are made here and it isn't a factory. It's actually a maze of unusual little shops selling work by local crafters and artists. You can buy novelty gifts and souvenirs.

3. Brown and Hopkins Country Store
📍 E4 🏠 1179 Putnam Pike, Chepachet 🌐 shopbrown andhopkins.com
Children can select from the "penny candy" counter while their parents browse the home furnishings and accessories at this historic store.

4. Bowen's Wharf
📍 F5 🏠 America's Cup Ave, Newport 🌐 bowenswharf.com
These 18th-century wharf shops sell a range of gifts and souvenirs, often with a nautical flavor.

5. Warren
📍 F4
If it's old, you'll probably find it here. A cluster of stores in this former whaling port have turned it into a collectors' hub.

6. Thames Glass
📍 F5 🏠 688 Thames St, Newport 🌐 thamesglass.com
Watch glassblowers in action at this studio, then visit the store for a finished piece. Visitors can also sign up to learn glassblowing from a skilled glassblower.

Display of students' design work at the RISD store

7. Peter Pots Pottery
📍 E5 🏠 494 Glen Rock Rd, West Kingston 🌐 peterpots.com
Collectors favor the modern lines and distinctive glazes of Peter Pots Pottery, founded in 1948. The studio, in an 18th-century mill building, displays the complete line of dinnerware and decorative pieces.

8. Pier Marketplace
📍 E5 🏠 Narragansett Town Beach, Narragansett
On breaks from the beach, sunbathers browse the resort wear and gift shops here, then treat themselves to ice cream or a bag of saltwater taffy.

9. Providence Place
📍 E4 🏠 1 Providence Place, Providence 🌐 providenceplace.com
This shopping mall in the heart of downtown Providence overlooks Waterfront Park and features every local and national chain store you could ask for.

10. Garden City Center
📍 E4 🏠 Rte 2, Cranston 🌐 gardencitycenter.com
Established in 1948, this outdoor village-like complex, 7 miles (11 km) from Providence, offers a wide range of shopping options. After a full day of shopping, visitors can rest their feet in the center's green area.

Cafés and Bars

Olympia Tea Room, a quaint bar in Watch Hill

1. Perks and Corks
📍 E5 🏠 62 High St, Westerly
ⓦ perksandcorks.com

A laid-back coffee bar by day – with smooth lattes, free Wi-Fi, and enveloping sofas – Perks and Corks morphs into a bar serving wines by the glass and killer cocktails after dark.

2. Chan's Fine Oriental Dining
📍 E3 🏠 267 Main St, Woonsocket
ⓦ chanseggrollsjazz.com

Known for its "eggroll jazz," Chan's comes alive on the weekends when blues bands and small jazz combos set the diners' fingers snapping.

3. 22 Bowen's Wine Bar and Grille
📍 F5 🏠 22 Bowen's Wharf, Newport
ⓦ 22bowens.com

Watch boat traffic in the harbor, while tucking into prime rib or slurping down oysters at this stylish spot, also known for its wines (there are over 600).

4. Café Zoey
📍 E4 🏠 791 Hope St, Providence
ⓦ cafezoey.com

A cheery morning spot, this café offers vegan muffins, sweet and savory crepes, and specialty coffees from a range of fair-traded sources.

5. Trinity Brewhouse
📍 E4 🏠 200 Washington St, Providence ⓦ clementinecocktailbar.com

A chic cocktail lounge in the heart of Providence, Clementine is famous for its innovative drinks. Its lively interior, with brick walls and modern art, is always abuzz with visitors.

6. Olympia Tea Room
📍 E5 🏠 74 Bay St, Watch Hill
ⓦ olympiatearoom.com

Score one of the outdoor tables at this delightful spot near the Flying Horses Carousel, and you can watch the action while you sip white wine and eat roasted clams with linguine.

7. Scales and Shells
📍 F5 🏠 527 Thames St, Newport
ⓦ scalesandshells.com

After the dinner rush, this all-fish restaurant turns into a convivial bar where patrons can enjoy local shellfish from the raw bar with a glass of wine or beer.

8. George's of Galilee
📍 E5 🏠 250 Sand Hill Cove Rd, Galilee ⓦ georgesofgalilee.com

Stop off here to savor the pick of the catch from the Galilee fishers; many spend their evenings at the bar.

9. Costantino's Venda Bar and Ristorante
📍 E4 🏠 265 Atwells Ave, Providence
ⓦ costantinosristorante.com

This Italian gourmet shop offers a huge array of pastas, cheeses, and sausages. You can enjoy food and coffee on-site.

10. McKinley's Waterfront
📍 E4 🏠 1 Division St, East Greenwich

This warm Irish pub is a welcome find on a cool winter night, thanks to over 20 ales on tap. In summer, its waterfront seating is an ideal spot to sip a brew and watch the sailboats cruise by.

Restaurants

1. White Horse Tavern
F5 · 26 Marlborough St, Newport · L · whitehorsenewport.com · $$
The US's oldest tavern – with beamed ceilings, log fires, and candlelit tables – offers classic American cuisine.

2. Le Central
F4 · 483 Hope St, Bristol · Mon · lecentralbristol.net · $$
Narragansett meets Paris at this French bistro with excellent comfort food, including great local fish.

3. Coast Guard House Restaurant
E5 · 140 Ocean Rd, Narragansett · thecoastguardhouse.com · $$
A waterfront property with a lovely patio, this restaurant has been serving local seafood since the 1940s.

4. Al Forno
E4 · 577 S. Main St, Providence · L Tue–Sat; Sun & Mon · alforno.com · $$$
Al Forno has a great reputation for its tasty baked pastas and meats roasted in a wood-fired oven.

5. Coast in Ocean House
E5 · 1 Bluff Ave, Westerly · L Sun, D Mon & Tue · oceanhouseri.com · $$$
The hotel restaurant's open kitchen allows diners to watch the chefs as they prepare elegant American dishes.

6. New Rivers
E4 · 7 Steeple St, Providence · L Sun–Tue · newriversrestaurant.com · $$
Spicy contemporary cooking at its best pairs with an intimate dining space for a truly romantic experience.

7. Giusto
F5 · 94 Commercial Wharf, Newport · L Mon–Fri · giustonewport.com · $$
The catch of the day competes with smoked brisket and a wide range of inventive pastas at this place.

8. Wright's Farm Restaurant
E4 · 84 Inman Rd, Harrisville · L Mon–Fri, D Mon–Wed · wrightsfarm.com · $
This 1,000-seater is the best of the Rhode Island "all-you-can-eat chicken dinner" restaurants. After their meal, diners can browse the restaurant's gift shop, which offers a wide array of jewelry, fashion accessories, gourmet candies, and specialty foods.

9. Restaurant 1879, Atlantic Inn
E6 · High St, Block Island · 401 466 5883 · L all year, D late Apr–late May & Sep–late Oct Mon–Wed · $$$
Fish and farm produce feature on the menu at this contemporary American eatery. The verandah tables offer spectacular views of the sunset.

10. Matunuck Oyster Bar
F4 · 629 Succotash Rd, Wakefield · rhodyoysters.com · $$
In a true farm-to-table experience, the oysters served here are farmed across the street at Potter's Pond. Fresh scallops and fin fish complete the menu.

Ocean House, home to the Coast restaurant

CONNECTICUT

The Connecticut River touches four states, but only gives its name to one. America's third-smallest state is beloved for its gently rolling countryside (picture sandy beaches, shady woods, and golden marshes), much of which was captured by the famed American Impressionists a century or so ago. This art movement isn't Connecticut's only claim to fame, however. The state is also home to one of America's most famous universities, Yale, which is surrounded by suitably academic institutions, including a renowned museum of natural history. Then there's the state capital, Hartford, which promises a wealth of historical sites, alongside popular local restaurants and sprawling green spaces.

1 Top 10 Sights *p103*
1 Fine Dining *p110*
1 Family Attractions *p106*
1 Cafés and Bars *p109*
1 Places to Shop *p108*
1 Gardens and House Museums *p106*
1 Casual Dining *p111*

Towering spire of the Connecticut State Capitol, Hartford

1 Hartford
☑ C4

As the state capital, Hartford has many grand buildings and institutions, from the Victorian-Gothic Connecticut State Capitol in Bushnell Park to the public art museum, Wadsworth Atheneum

(p49), founded in 1842. Hartford was also a hotbed of 19th-century publishing and writing. The Mark Twain House *(p52)*, where one of America's greatest storytellers and frontier humorists enjoyed a later life of middle-class comfort, and the Gothic-Revival-style Harriet Beecher Stowe Center *(p106)* next door, underscores the city's literary prominence. Smell the roses – more than 800 varieties of them – in Elizabeth Park, home to a 1904-era garden *(p106)*.

2 Quiet Corner
☑ D4

The unassuming nickname for Connecticut's northeastern corner suggests that little of excitement has happened here since General Israel Putnam killed the last wolf in the state, and made it safe for sheep-farming. In truth, this area of bucolic repose is dotted with the homes of former country squires, including the flamboyant Roseland Cottage Bowen House *(p106)*. The region is often overlooked, but antiques hunters always stop in Putnam *(p108)*.

3 Wethersfield
☑ C4

Preserved within a 12-block area, Old Wethersfield stands as a primer of American architecture, with numerous houses from the 18th to 20th centuries, including three buildings that depict the differing lifestyles of three 18th-century Americans (a wealthy merchant, a diplomat, and a leather tanner), and form the Webb-Deane-Stevens Museum *(webb-deane-stevens.org)*.

Exhibit at Yale Peabody Museum of Natural History, New Haven

4 New Haven
☑ C5

Home to the prestigious Yale University, New Haven is credited as being one of the first planned cities in the US. Collections at the Yale University Art Museums *(p50)* and the Yale Peabody Museum of Natural History *(peabody.yale.edu)* put larger cities to shame. The town's culinary legacy includes the legendary pizzas of Frank Pepe *(p111)*.

5 New London and Groton
☑ D5

The deepwater port at the mouth of the Thames River – Groton on the east side, New London on the west – lies roughly halfway between Boston and New York. It was a key base of operations for the American Navy during the Revolution; nowadays, ocean cruise ships call here. The massive shipyards of Electric Boat, builder of nuclear-powered submarines, are in Groton. Explore the Submarine Force Museum *(p55)*, home of the world's first nuclear-powered sub, the USS *Nautilus*.

6 Lower Connecticut River
☑ D5

Designated as a "last great place" by the Nature Conservancy, the lower reaches of the Connecticut River, from East Haddam to Lyme, have a magical beauty that captivates artists and sustains fish and wildlife, including large numbers of bald eagles in the winter. See how the American Impressionists captured the scene at the Florence Griswold Museum *(p106)* in Old Lyme, and explore the rich history and fascinating ecology of the region at the Connecticut River Museum *(ctrivermuseum.org)*.

7 Gold Coast
☑ B6

The communities that lie along the New Haven commuter rail line from Greenwich north to Norwalk are the wealthiest in Connecticut – hence the nickname "Gold Coast." When residents want to shop, they head to Greenwich, where boutiques cater to hedge fund millionaires. To dine or to party, they usually make a beeline for South Norwalk, where a bustling bar and restaurant scene has taken hold.

8 Midcoast Beaches
☑ C6

The great shield of Long Island shelters the sandy shoreline between New Haven Harbor and the mouth of the

Connecticut River at Old Lyme. Protected from storms and erosion, the barrier beaches feature soft sand and gentle surf. Many private beach communities are located here, but so are the main state-owned beaches, which include the 2-mile (3-km) strand at Hammonasset Beach State Park (*p60*). Communities like Branford and Clinton live for the sweet but brief summer (stores are often seasonal).

9 Mystic and Stonington
D5 & E5

Small seafaring ports of the eastern Connecticut coast, Stonington and Mystic (*p105*) diverged when the latter (home to the re-created Mystic Seaport village) developed as a tourism center. Quieter Stonington, 4 miles (6.5 km) away, retains all the hallmarks of a 19th-century fishing and shipping port, and is dotted with upscale boutiques, cheery cafés, and bars.

10 Litchfield Hills

Stretching westward from the Connecticut River to the New York border, the Litchfield Hills are Connecticut's manicured mountains. Model 18th- and 19th-century communities of white houses and churches cluster around tidy town greens. In spring, waterfalls roar off the hillsides and you'll find hardy anglers wading cold mountain brooks to cast flies for trout. In summer, the smell of newly mown lawns and the sweet scents of flower gardens perfume the air.

Housatonic River in the Litchfield Hills

A DRIVING TOUR FROM TALL SHIPS TO SUBMARINES

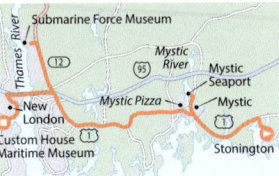

Morning

Begin the day by exploring the picturesque fishing and erstwhile shipping village of **Stonington**. Many a tall ship for whaling and overseas trade was constructed along the Mystic River here. To get more of a feel for those maritime days, drive downriver 4 miles (6.5 km) to the village of **Mystic** (which is half in Groton, half in Stonington). Spend the rest of the morning exploring the vessels and the re-created village of **Mystic Seaport** (*p54*). Make sure you tour the *Charles W. Morgan*, the last surviving wooden whaling ship.

Afternoon

Indulge in delicious pizza from **Mystic Pizza** (*56 W Main St*) and follow Rte 1 west through the coastal plain to the **Submarine Force Museum** (*p55*). This is where the American nuclear-powered submarine program unfolded after World War II. Tour the first vessel (the USS *Nautilus*) and try your hand at the simulated controls of a complex modern submarine. Just across the Thames River lies the historic town of **New London** (*p56*), where you can continue your maritime-themed tour at the **Custom House Maritime Museum** (*150 Bank St*), which also offers visitors lighthouse tours and boat trips.

Gardens and House Museums

Flowers in bloom at the Elizabeth Park Rose Gardens

1. Roseland Cottage Bowen House

🅟 D4 🏠 556 Rte 169, Woodstock
🕐 Jun–mid-Oct: Thu–Sun
🆆 historicnewengland.org ↗

This pink, Gothic-style cottage was the summer getaway for the wealthy Bowen family of New York.

2. Bush-Holley Historic Site

🅟 A6 🏠 39 Strickland Rd, Cos Cob
🕐 For tours: noon, 1:30pm, & 3pm Wed–Sun 🆆 greenwichhistory.org ↗↗

This expanded and modernized site pinpoints two revolutions: the political upheaval of the 1770s and the artistic ferment of American Impressionism, 125 years later.

3. Bartlett Arboretum

🅟 A6 🏠 151 Brookdale Rd, Stamford
🕐 Dawn–dusk 🆆 bartlettarboretum.org

Woodlands, wetlands, meadows, and formal gardens make a living museum of 850 specimen trees.

4. Florence Griswold Museum

🅟 D5 🏠 96 Lyme St, Old Lyme 🕐 Mon
🆆 florencegriswoldmuseum.org ↗

View the history of American Impressionism at this former rooming house, where artist-boarders painted more than 40 panels on the walls.

5. Elizabeth Park Rose Gardens

🅟 C4 🏠 Asylum Ave, Hartford
🕐 Daily 🆆 elizabethparkct.org

Built on land donated by Charles M. Pond in honor of his wife, this is the oldest municipal rose garden in the US. It features 800 varieties of roses.

6. Hill-Stead Museum

🅟 C4 🏠 35 Mountain Rd, Farmington
🕐 Mon & Tue 🆆 hillstead.org ↗

This hilltop estate is an aristocratic world of privilege, renowned for its French Impressionist paintings and architecture.

7. Glebe House Museum and Gertrude Jekyll Garden

🅟 B5 🏠 49 Hollow Rd, Woodbury
🕐 May–early Oct: Fri–Sun
🆆 glebehousemuseum.org ↗

This 1750 home has the only US garden created by famed British designer Gertrude Jekyll.

8. Lockwood-Mathews Mansion Museum

🅟 B6 🏠 295 West Ave, Norwalk
🕐 Wed–Sun (guided tours only)
🆆 lochwoodmathewsmansion.com ↗

Decorative excesses abound at this estate, built for a wealthy banker and railroad tycoon.

9. Harriet Beecher Stowe Center

🅟 C4 🏠 77 Forest St, Hartford
🕐 Wed–Sat 🆆 harrietbeecher stowecenter.org ↗

Harriet Beecher Stowe, author of famed novel *Uncle Tom's Cabin*, moved here, her last home, in 1873.

10. Bellamy-Ferriday House and Garden

🅟 B4 🏠 9 Main St N, Bethlehem
🕐 Hours vary, check website
🆆 ctlandmarks.org ↗

Built by Reverend Joseph Bellamy in the 18th century, this property's final owner was philanthropist Carolyn W. Ferriday.

Family Attractions

1. Connecticut's Beardsley Zoo
🏛 B6 🏠 1875 Noble Ave, Bridgeport
🕐 Daily 🌐 beardsleyzoo.org 🔗
Siberian tigers are the top cats at this 300-animal zoo. Take a peak at the wolves from the observation area.

2. International Skating Center of Connecticut (ISCC)
🏛 C4 🏠 1375 Hopmeadow St, Simsbury 🕐 Hours vary, chech website 🌐 isccskate.com 🔗
A world-class skating facility with twin rinks, this center is a training ground for many Olympic skaters and is also open for public skating.

3. Maritime Aquarium at Norwalk
🏛 B6 🏠 10 N Water St, Norwalk
🕐 Daily 🌐 maritimeaquarium.org 🔗
This aquatic center highlights the creatures in its own backyard, like harbor seals and sand tiger sharks.

4. Conneticut Science Center
🏛 C4 🏠 250 Columbus Blvd, Hartford 🕐 Daily
🌐 ctsciencecenter.org 🔗
Gripping environmental exhibits dominate this nine-level museum set on Connecticut River banks.

5. Mashantucket Pequot Museum
🏛 D5 🏠 110 Pequot Trail, Mashantucket 🕐 Wed–Sat (Nov: Tue–Sat) 🌐 pequotmuseum.org 🔗
This museum, dedicated to Indigenous culture, is run by the Mashantucket Pequot Tribal Nation. It recounts the area's history from the perspective of its pre-colonial inhabitants.

6. Ocean Beach Park
🏛 D5 🏠 98 Neptune Ave, New London 🕐 Late May–early Sep
🌐 ocean-beach-park.com 🔗
A veritable paradise for children, this beach park promises a great day out.

7. The Dinosaur Place
🏛 D5 🏠 1650 Rte 85, Montville
🕐 9:30am–6pm daily
🌐 thedinosaurplace.com 🔗
Every child loves a dinosaur, and over 40 life-sized concrete dinosaurs wait to be discovered here, along nature trails through lush woodlands.

8. Essex Steam Train and Riverboat
🏛 D5 🏠 1 Railroad Ave, Essex 🕐 May–Oct 🌐 essexsteamtrain.com 🔗
Experience a diesel-train simulator, before riding a vintage train and a riverboat along the Connecticut River on this historic railroad.

9. New England Air Museum
🏛 C4 🏠 36 Perimeter Rd, Bradley International Airport, Windsor Locks
🕐 9am–4pm daily 🌐 neam.org 🔗
Marvel at 65 aircrafts and numerous fascinating airplane models that are on display here. The museum's library is a haven for aviation enthusiasts, with 6,000 books on the subject.

10. Carousel Museum
🏛 C4 🏠 95 Riverside Dr, Bristol 🕐 Wed–Sun 🌐 thecarouselmuseum.org 🔗
This museum features carousel carvings and amazing art that spans a century. It also offers a Venetian carousel for children. There are interactive labs, which provide visitors with a hands-on experience in building a carousel, too.

Aircraft at the New England Air Museum

Extravagant interior of The Shops at Mohegan Sun

Places to Shop

1. "The Avenue," Greenwich
📍 A6
Greenwich is the "platinum" town on Connecticut's Gold Coast, and Greenwich Avenue is packed with luxury boutiques to feather the finest nest.

2. Guilford Art Center
📍 C5 🏠 411 Church St, Guilford
🌐 guilfordartcenter.org
Guildford bustles each July with a juried exhibition of fine crafts. But this center promotes crafts year-round, with classes and a shop full of unique hand-crafted items.

3. Woodbury Pewter
📍 B5 🏠 860 Main St S, Woodbury
🌐 woodburypewter.com
You could discover the perfect candlestick, bowl, or teapot at a discounted price at the factory outlet of this family-owned company.

4. The Shops at Mohegan Sun
📍 D5 🏠 1 Mohegan Sun Blvd, Uncasville 🌐 mohegansun.com
This casino complex features upscale shops, offering everything from high-end fashion to handmade cosmetics.

5. Westfarms Mall, West Hartford
📍 C3 🏠 1500 New Britain Ave, West Hartford 🌐 shopwestfarms.com
A popular shopping mall, with over 160 ritzy stores, Westfarms offers a wide range of products, from clothing to gadgets.

6. Olde Mistick Village
📍 D5 🏠 Coogan Blvd, Mystic
🌐 oldemistichvillage.com
Enjoy the lush gardens, a duck pond, and a waterwheel accent at this complex not far from the Mystic Seaport (p54).

7. Artisan's Marketplace
📍 C4 🏠 120 East St, Plainville
🌐 artisansmarketplacect.com
Over 400 studio artists working with jewelry, pottery, glass, wood, and fibers display their work here.

8. Chapel St, New Haven
📍 C5
Chapel Street skirts the edge of the Yale campus with stores catering to faculty and students alike. Look for designer clothing boutiques and bookstore cafés.

9. Putnam
📍 D4 🏠 Antiques Marketplace: 109 Main St
The Antiques Marketplace, established in a former department store, has revitalized what was once a former mill town. If you're searching for a specific collectible and don't find it here, be sure to explore the town's smaller shops.

10. Clinton Crossing Premium Outlets
📍 C5 🏠 20-A Killingworth Turnpike, Clinton 🌐 premiumoutlets.com
Enjoy good discounts here on designer wear at over 70 stores, including Calvin Klein, Kate Spade, Saks Fifth Avenue, and Vera Bradley.

Cafés and Bars

1. Max's Oyster Bar
C4 964 Farmington Ave, West Hartford 11:30am–9pm Thu–Sun (to 10pm Fri & Sat) maxsoysterbar.com

Showmanlike presentation of raw bar offerings sets the tone for this polished, dressy seafood joint.

2. New Park Brewing
C4 485 New Park Ave, West Hartford newparkbrewing.com

Located outside town, this brewery is loved for its craft beers and home-made pizzas. There's live music, too.

3. Toad's Place
C5 300 York St, New Haven toadsplace.com

One of the state's biggest dance floors and a sound system that could rock a stadium make Toad's the "ultimate" dance venue on Saturday nights.

4. White Hart Provisions
B4 15 Undermountain Rd, Salisbury whitehartinn.com

This small café housed in an old inn doubles up as a grocery store and an espresso bar. The coffee is excellent and there are plenty of breakfast and lunch options to choose from.

5. Water Street Café
E5 143 Water St, Stonington waterstcafe.com

Locals favor Water Street for great oysters at the raw bar, chilled white wine, and live guitar music, but don't overlook dishes like the lobster spring rolls or the warm duck salad.

6. @ the Corner
B4 3 West St, Litchfield athecorner.com

This former bakery offers a delicious array of soups, salads, and sandwiches at lunchtime. In the evenings, there's a great range of craft beer and bar fare on the menu.

7. Little Pub
A6 531 E Putnam Ave, Cos Cob littlepub.com

Burgers and beer are the mainstays of this relaxed bar in the arty corner of Greenwich. Variants of mac and cheese are menu staples.

8. SONO Sky Bar
B6 45 S. Main St, Norwalk sonoshybarnorwalk.com

This busy rooftop bar in trendy Norwalk has a nautical theme. Expect good wine, beer, and well-curated cocktails.

9. Armada Brewing
C5 190 River St, New Haven armadabrewing.com

A popular local brewery, Armada Brewing offers a wide variety of craft beers, ales, and ciders, but a small selection of food choices. Bingo nights are held every Thursday.

10. Wine Bar at the Griswold Inn
D5 36 Main St, Essex griswoldinn.com

This intimate bar offers a good selection of mature cheeses and tapas-style platters paired with excellent wines.

Stylish decor of Max's Oyster Bar

Fine Dining

1. Oyster Club
D5 ▢ 13 Water St, Mystic ▢ Mon–Thu L ▢ oysterclubct.com · $$

This restaurant and raw bar specializes in fresh seafood and features a menu that showcases produce from local farms and fish from nearby ports.

2. Union League Café
C5 ▢ 1032 Chapel St, New Haven ▢ Sun & Mon ▢ unionleaguecafe.com · $$$

The French chef-owner of Union League brings the hearty, market-driven cuisine of a Parisian brasserie to the sophisticated streets of New Haven near Yale University.

3. Max Downtown
C4 ▢ City Place, 185 Asylum St, Hartford ▢ L Sat & Sun ▢ maxdowntown.com · $$$

Tasty beef ranges from petite steak *au poivre* to giant porterhouse at this bustling urban chophouse.

4. Metro Bis
C4 ▢ 4690 Hopmeadow Rd, Simsbury ▢ Sun & Mon ▢ metrobis.com · $$$

Set in an elegant mansion, this modern bistro serves fresh, light meals made with local ingredients. Dinner is generally a modestly priced three-course affair. It also has a good wine selection.

5. 85 Main
D4 ▢ 85 Main St, Putnam ▢ 85main.com · $$

Sample the superb seafood in either the cozy dining room or the blue-and-white tiled bar of this restaurant.

6. Hopkins Inn
B4 ▢ 22 Hopkins Rd, New Preston ▢ Tue–Sun (Jan–late Mar: Tue–Sat) ▢ thehopkinsinn.com · $$

The menu is laden with Austrian fare such as *schnitzel* and sweetbreads. The wine selection follows suit.

7. Good News Restaurant and Bar
B5 ▢ 694 Main St S, Woodbury ▢ 11:30am–9:30pm Thu–Sun (to 10pm Fri & Sat) ▢ goodnewswoodbury.com · $$

The chef-owner insists on only local, sustainable, organic products, but her food is never precious, just delicious.

8. Match
B6 ▢ 98 Washington St, S Norwalk ▢ L Mon & Tue ▢ matchsono.com · $$

Sparkling seafood dishes, inventive seasonal fare, and rich desserts are a perfect match to the hippest bar on SoNo's restaurant row.

9. Todd English's Tuscany
D5 ▢ 1 Mohegan Sun Blvd, Uncasville ▢ 860 862 3236 · $$

Rustic environs and celebrity chef Todd English's expertly executed Tuscan flavors are the highlight here.

10. Rocks 21 Restaurant
D5 ▢ Inn at Mystic, 3 Williams Ave, Mystic ▢ rocks21.com · $$

Classic seafood, wood-fired pizzas, a great raw bar, and craft beer make this waterfront dining room a local favorite.

The picture-perfect exterior of Oyster Club

Casual Dining

PRICE CATEGORIES
For a three-course meal for one with half a bottle of wine (or equivalent meal), taxes and extra charges.
....
$ under $45 **$$** $45–$80 **$$$** over $80

Memorabilia-filled counter at the famous Mystic Pizza

1. Frank Pepe Pizzeria Napoletana
C5 ☐157 Wooster St, New Haven
☐ pepespizzeria.com · **$**
The thin-crust pizza at this no-frills joint open since 1925 has an almost cult following among Yale students. White clam pizza (no tomato sauce) is among the most popular.

2. Bear's Smokehouse Barbecue
C4 ☐25 Front St, Hartford
☐ bearsbbq.com · **$$**
Savor burnt ends, sweet-potato mash, and ribs at this local BBQ joint owned by Jamie "Bear" McDonald.

3. Rawley's Drive-In
B6 ☐1886 Post Rd, Rte 1, Fairfield ☐11am–7pm Mon–Sat ☐ rawleysdrivein.com · **$**
When customers are willing to wait in line for hours, it's clear a restaurant is doing something right. It's the hot dogs that keep them coming back for more.

4. Marlborough Tavern
D4 ☐3 E. Hampton Rd, Marlborough ☐L Wed–Fri, Mon & Tue ☐ marlboroughtavernct.com · **$$**
This former stagecoach tavern established in 1760 serves casual American bar food, but is best known for its innovative cocktails.

5. Captain Scott's Lobster Dock
D5 ☐80 Hamilton St, New London
☐Apr–mid-Oct: 11am–6pm daily
☐ captscotts.com · **$**
Known for its hot lobster rolls with butter and lobster salad, this seafood shack has quality few can match.

6. Mystic Pizza
D5 ☐56 W Main St, Mystic
☐ mysticpizza.com · **$**
Julia Roberts' eponymous movie made this pizza-and-pasta joint famous, but diners keep returning for the "secret recipe" tomato sauce that's generously slathered on the pizzas.

7. Shady Glen
C4 ☐840 E Middle Turnpike, Manchester ☐860 649 4245 · **$**
The homemade ice cream is great, but it's the cheeseburger that is really the top star here.

8. Blackie's Hot Dog Stand
C5 ☐2200 Waterbury Rd, Cheshire ☐ blackieshotdogs.com ☐Fri · **$**
Since 1928, Blackie's has offered hot dogs with homemade spicy relish, birch beer on tap, and chocolate milk.

9. Rein's
C4 ☐435 Hartford Turnpike, Vernon ☐ reinsdeli.com · **$**
Rein's makes better Jewish deli food, including *latkes*, than most of New York, and is just off highway I-84.

10. West Street Grill
B4 ☐43 West St, Litchfield
☐ weststreetgrill.com · **$$**
Casual lunches are a big hit here, especially the burgers and the pulled short-rib beef sandwich.

VERMONT

Lacking an ocean coastline, Vermont stretches across the spectacular Green Mountains range from Lake Champlain eastward to the Connecticut River. Black-and-white dairy cows graze its hillside pastures, while pretty villages with high-steepled white churches nestle in sheltered valleys. The largest city, Burlington, is a foodie hot-spot with a lively music scene and active lifestyle – perfectly placed on the shores of Lake Champlain for swimming, boating, and cycling along the waterfront. And there are plenty more outdoor activities on offer here; despite severe winter weather, Vermonters are outdoors year-round, hiking, skiing, skating, sledding, and fishing.

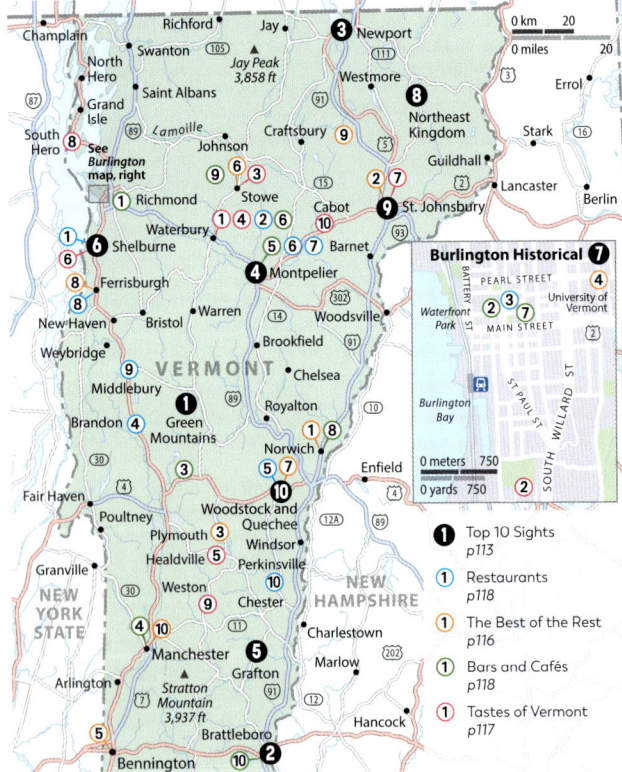

① Top 10 Sights
p113

① Restaurants
p118

① The Best of the Rest
p116

① Bars and Cafés
p118

① Tastes of Vermont
p117

For places to stay in this area, see p150

1 Green Mountains

It would scarcely be an exaggeration to say that Vermont is the Green Mountains *(p40)* and vice versa, as this ancient range in the Appalachian chain touches almost every part of the state.

2 Brattleboro

🗺 **K6**

Vermont's first permanent English settlement, Brattleboro flourished in the 19th century as a Connecticut River manufacturing town at the juncture of Vermont, Massachusetts, and New Hampshire. The town got a new lease on life in the 1960s as the counterculture capital of the upper Connecticut River Valley, and is known around the state for its stridently liberal politics. The thriving cultural community includes several galleries, a performing arts center, and a school of circus arts that is open to the general public. Brattleboro was named in the book *The 100 Best Small Art Towns in America* by John Villani.

Vermont State Capitol building in Montpelier

3 Newport

🗺 **L5**

Vermont's northernmost city is set at the southern edge of Lake Memphremagog, a body of water 27 miles (43 km) long that is shared with the province of Quebec. A glacial lake that was a saltwater inland sea at the end of the Laurentian glaciation, Memphremagog has long been rumored to hold a sea serpent akin to the Loch Ness Monster. Sightings of the elusive creature that locals call "Memphre" date to the 18th century. Take a stroll along the attractive waterfront and see if you can spy those watery coils from the safety of the shore.

4 Montpelier

🗺 **K3**

For an iconic Vermont image, stop along State Street during foliage season to take a picture with the gold-domed State House backed by a hillside of red and flame-orange maple trees. The city was selected for state capital in 1805 because it lies at the geographic center of Vermont as well as in the main east-west pass through the Green Mountains. Today Montpelier has a thriving home-grown acoustic-music scene, and restaurants reliant on local farm products.

Cheeses on display at Grafton Village Cheese Company

ETHAN ALLEN

Vermont folk figure Ethan Allen (1738–89) led a militia called the Green Mountain Boys. He rebuffed colonial governors and British troops alike in a quest for Vermont's independence. His capture of Fort Ticonderoga from British forces in 1775 played a key strategic role early in the American Revolution.

5 Grafton
K6

Wealthy philanthropists saved this beautiful village in the 1960s by forming the Windham Foundation to restore its handsome buildings and revitalize commerce. Today, it's a lovely spot for some shopping: pick up a sweet treat at the Plummer's Sugar House (*plummerssugarhouse.com*), a third-generation maple syrup farm; or purchase Vermont's famous cheese at the Grafton Village Cheese Company (*graftonvillagecheese.com*) or at old-school general store, MKT Grafton (*mktgrafton.com*). Come evening the 1801 tavern in the Grafton Inn *(grafton innvermont.com)* is great for dinner.

6 Shelburne
J3

Standing on high banks above Lake Champlain just south of Burlington, Shelburne is a village of magnificent dairy farms, not least among them the historic spread of Shelburne Farms *(p117)*. The 2.2-sq-mile (5.7-sq-km) former farmhouse is an elegant seasonal inn with a celebrated restaurant *(p119)*. The Shelburne Museum *(p49)* has extensive collections of quilts, weathervanes, and other folk art. The museum grounds also feature a locomotive, a steamship, and a covered bridge.

7 Burlington
J3

Settled shortly before the American Revolution, Burlington, unlike the rest of Vermont, takes its identity less from the Green Mountains than from the great inland sea of Lake Champlain. Burlington shipyards turned timber into trading vessels. Visitors can learn about the region's history on the Lake Champlain Cruise *(p62)*. Blessed with a handsome, largely 19th-century downtown, Burlington enjoys a busy cultural life thanks to the presence of the state university *(uvm.edu)*.

8 Northeast Kingdom
L2

"Northeast Kingdom" refers to Essex, Orleans, and Caledonia counties in the state's northeast corner – an area

Lake Wiloughby's fall foliage, Northeast Kingdom

sometimes referred to simply as "The Kingdom." With only two large communities, St. Johnsbury and Newport, it is one of the most rural parts of the state. The area is known for skiing, stunning fall foliage, and maple syrup.

9 St. Johnsbury
⑨ L3

"St. J," as Vermonters call it, is both the hub of the state's Northeast Kingdom and the gateway between Vermont and New Hampshire. When Thaddeus Fairbanks invented the platform scale in 1830, the town became his manu-facturing center. The Fairbanks clan donated both the Fairbanks Museum and Planetarium *(p116)*, and the Athenaeum *(stjathenaeum.org)*, a library and gallery.

10 Woodstock and Quechee
⑦ K5

It's little wonder that Woodstock is such a popular destination for weddings. With its broad town green, restored Federal and Victorian houses, covered bridges, and five churches with Paul Revere bells, it is the very picture of old-time Vermont. Even the Billings Farm *(p46)* showcases Vermont rural life. Head east on Route 4 to see the Quechee Gorge carved by the Ottauquechee River.

A DAY IN ROBERT FROST COUNTRY

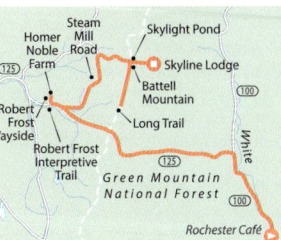

Rochester Café

Morning

Robert Frost (1874–1963), the seminal poet of the New England countryside, spent 39 summers near the **Green Mountain National Forest** *(p40)*. This day of hiking and driving explores the area he loved. Start with pancakes and maple syrup at the **Rochester Café** *(rochestercafe. com)*, at the same soda fountain where Frost used to eat, and have the café pack you a lunch. Then, drive west on Rte 125 to the **Robert Frost Interpretive Trail**, where you can read some of Frost's verse and learn to identify native plants. Just east of the **Robert Frost Wayside** *(p41)* picnic area, a five-minute walk on a dirt road will bring you to Frost's cabin at the **Homer Noble Farm**, maintained as he left it.

Afternoon

When inspiration evaded Frost, he sought solace in the woods. For a hike, drive east on Rte 125 and turn left onto **Steam Mill Road**. Park at the **Skylight Pond** trailhead. The path ascends the flank of **Battell Mountain**, crisscrossing the hillside through a forest of white birch, red oak, and hemlocks. The moderate 90-minute climb ends on a ridge connecting to the legendary **Long Trail** *(p41)*. Turn left for a hike to **Skyline Lodge**, a shelter for hikers.

The Best of the Rest

1. Montshire Museum

L4 ▪ 1 Montshire Rd, Norwich
▪ montshire.org

This 110-acre (44-ha) museum features over 150 exhibits covering astronomy, nature, and technology. Its outdoor trails are a favorite among children.

2. Fairbanks Museum and Planetarium

L3 ▪ 1302 Main St, St. Johnsbury
▪ 10am–5pm daily ▪ fairbanks museum.org

Set up in 1889 by Franklin Fairbanks, this museum is a treasure trove for kids. Hands-on exhibits make for an exciting visit.

3. President Calvin Coolidge State Historic Site

K5 ▪ 3780 Rte 100A, Plymouth
▪ Late May–mid-Oct: Tue–Sun
▪ historicsites.vermont.gov

The childhood home of the 30th US president, this is also the place where Coolidge took the oath of office.

4. Fleming Museum of Art

J3 ▪ 61 Colchester Ave, Burlington
▪ Hours vary, chech website
▪ uvm.edu/fleming

Artifacts including Nigerian Yoruba statues, medieval manuscripts, and Andy Warhol prints are displayed here.

Playing with a bubble at the Montshire Museum

5. Bennington Museum and Grandma Moses Gallery

J6 ▪ 75 Main St, Bennington
▪ Wed & Jan–Mar ▪ bennington museum.org

Stop by and browse this major collection of work by folk artist Grandma Moses.

6. Vermont Ski and Snowboard Museum (VTSSM)

K3 ▪ 1 S. Main St, Stowe ▪ Mon–Wed ▪ vtssm.com

The VTSSM chronicles the history of skiing in the state, from the introduction of powered lifts to the present day.

7. Vermont Institute of Natural Science

K5 ▪ 149 Natures Way (off Rte 4), Quechee ▪ vinsweb.org

Dedicated to avian rehabilitation, this institute also spreads awareness about the environment.

8. Rokeby Museum

J3 ▪ 334 US-7, Ferrisburgh
▪ Mid-May–late Oct: daily
▪ rokeby.org

This farmstead and museum, with buildings including a smokehouse, hen house, and creamery, played a key role in the Underground Railroad.

9. Bread and Puppet Museum

L6 ▪ R753 Heights Rd, Glover
▪ 9am–6pm daily ▪ breadand puppet.org

Browse the huge collection of puppets, masks, props, and paintings belonging to this radical street theater company.

10. American Museum of Fly Fishing

K6 ▪ 4070 Main St, Manchester
▪ Hours vary, chech website
▪ amff.org

Exhibits such as rods, reels, and flies, some of which date to the 16th century, tell the story of angling in the US.

Entrance of The Vermont Country Store

Tastes of Vermont

1. Cold Hollow Cider Mill
K3 **3600 Waterbury-Stowe Rd, Rte 100, Waterbury Center** **Mill: 8am–6pm daily** **coldhollow.com**
Packed with Vermont specialties, this store is famous for its cider doughnuts and freshly pressed cider.

2. Lake Champlain Chocolates
J3 **750 Pine St, Burlington** **Hours vary, chech website** **lakechamplainchocolates.com**
The flagship store of the decadent chocolate brand features a giant collection of chocolate sculptures.

3. The Alchemist Brewery
K3 **100 Cottage Club Rd, Stowe** **11am–8pm daily** **alchemistbeer.com**
Specializing in unfiltered IPAs, this family-run brewery attracts a loyal fanbase to its beer garden.

4. Ben and Jerry's Ice Cream Factory
K3 **Rte 100, Waterbury** **benjerry.com**
Churning out mouth-watering ice-cream, this is the only Ben and Jerry's factory open to the public.

5. Crowley Cheese Co.
K5 **14 Crowley Ln, Healdville** **8am–4pm Mon–Fri, 10am–5pm Sat, 11am–5pm Sun** **crowleycheese.com**
Established in 1882, this is Vermont's oldest cheese factory, noted for its prize-winning Colby cheese.

6. Shelburne Farms
J3 **1611 Harbor Rd, Shelburne** **shelburnefarms.org**
This 1,400-acre (570-ha) farm, overlooking Lake Champlain, focuses on sustainable cultivation. Guided tours are available from May to October.

7. Maple Grove Farms Maple Museum and Gift Shop
L3 **1052 Portland St, St. Johnsbury** **Hours vary, chech website** **maplegrove.com**
Learn how tree sap is converted into a breakfast favorite and try the iconic tooth-tingling maple-leaf candies.

8. Snow Farm Vineyard
J2 **190 W Shore Rd, South Hero** **11am–5pm Thu–Sun, 11am–6pm Fri & Sat** **snowfarm.com**
Established in 1996, Snow Farm is Vermont's first vineyard and winery. It is particularly known for its distinctive Vidal Blanc ice wine.

9. The Vermont Country Store
K5 **657 Main St, Weston** **vermontcountrystore.com**
This emporium still has a pickle barrel and huge wedges of cheddar. Try its own Vermont Common Crackers.

10. Farmers' Store
L3 **2567 Waterbury-Stowe Rd** **Sun & Mon** **cabotcheese.com**
Vermont's largest cheese producer stocks a wide range of products such as butter, dips, spreads, and yogurt.

Cafés and Bars

1. Higher Ground
◉ J3 ⬕ 1214 Williston Rd, S. Burlington
ⓦ highergroundmusic.com
This top music venue features three bars and hosts a diverse lineup, from chart-topping artists to indie bands.

2. Drink
◉ J3 ⬕ 135 St. Paul St, Burlington
ⓦ drinkbarvermont.com
This sophisticated northern Vermont bar offers splashy mojitos and a selection of home-infused vodkas.

3. McGrath's Irish Pub
◉ K5 ⬕ Inn at Long Trail, 709 Rte 4, Sherburne Pass, Killington ⓦ innatlong trail.com/mcgraths-irish-pub
Darts, Guinness on draft, and live music on weekends await the loyal following at this amiable pub.

4. The Silver Fork
◉ K6 ⬕ 48 West Rd, Manchester Village ⓦ thesilverforkvt.com
Housed in a former village library, this stylish café serves international fare with French and Caribbean flavors.

5. Three Penny Taproom
◉ K3 ⬕ 108 Main St, Montpelier
ⓦ threepennytaproom.com
Home of the craft-beer movement in Vermont, this cool bar also serves simple bistro fare at bargain prices.

Wood-paneled interior of The Silver Fork

6. Prohibition Pig
◉ K3 ⬕ 23 S. Main St, Waterbury
ⓦ prohibitionpig.com
This friendly local hangout whips up classic cocktails alongside Vermont's most acclaimed craft beers. Delicious barbecue fare and a gluten-free menu keep the patrons satisfied.

7. Muddy Waters
◉ J3 ⬕ 184 Main St, Burlington
☎ 802 652 0466
A venerable coffee house with excellent expresso, local bagels and pastries. Muddy Waters also hosts occasional live music events.

8. Jasper Murdock's Alehouse
◉ L4 ⬕ 325 Main St, Norwich
ⓦ norwichinn.com/dining
This cozy pub brews its own English-style ales. It attracts large numbers of students from nearby Dartmouth College, as well as local ski buffs.

9. Matterhorn
◉ K3 ⬕ 4969 Mountain Rd, Stowe
ⓦ matterhornbar.com
The first bar south of Mount Mansfield is the perfect party stop after a day of skiing. Sushi dominates the menu, but the burgers are good, too.

10. Mocha Joe's Café
◉ K6 ⬕ 82 Main St, Brattleboro
This Brattleboro café is a popular spot for local artists and musicians, offering signature maple lattes and limeade.

Restaurants

Enjoying a meal at
American Flatbread

1. Inn at Shelburne Farms Restaurant

◻ J3 ◻ 1611 Harbor Rd, Shelburne
◻ L, mid-Oct–mid-May ◻ shelburne
farms.org · $$

This elegant dining room makes the
most of northern Vermont's short but
high-grade harvest, from early lettuces
to fall apples. It offers a special brunch
menu on Sundays.

2. Hen of the Wood

◻ K3 ◻ 14 S. Main St, Waterbury
◻ L ◻ henofthewood.com · $$

Plates here embody the essence of
gastronomic Vermont: local meats,
seasonal farm vegetables, foraged
foods, and exquisite cheeses.

3. Farmhouse Tap and Grill

◻ J3 ◻ 160 Bank St, Burlington
◻ farmhousetg.com · $$

Gourmet burgers, craft beer, and
dinner plates laden with Vermont
farm produce make Farmhouse a
local favorite.

4. Café Provence

◻ K4 ◻ 111 Center St, Brandon ◻ Mon
& Tue ◻ cafeprovencevt.com · $$

This restaurant's Provençal chef uses
Vermont produce to create traditional
French country cuisine served in an
intimate village bistro.

5. The Mill at Simon Pearce

◻ K5 ◻ 1760 Quechee Main
St, Quechee ◻ Mon ◻ simon
pearce.com · $$$

Savor the riverside location, superb
food, and fine wine at the Mill. Pearce, a
famed glass artist, has a studio on site.

6. Hugo's Bar and Grill

◻ K3 ◻ 44 Main St, Montpelier ◻ Sun
& Mon ◻ hugosbarandgrill.com · $$

Bistro classics such as mussels,
burgers, Philly beef, and maple
crème brûlée are on the menu here.

7. Oakes and Evelyn

◻ K3 ◻ 52 State St, Montpelier ◻ Sun
& Mon ◻ oakesandevelyn.com · $$

Located in downtown Montpelier, this
restaurant has a modern farm-to-table
menu with an array of veggie dishes.

8. Starry Night Café

◻ J3 ◻ 5371 Rte 7, Ferrisburgh ◻ L, Mon
& Tue ◻ starrynightcafe.com · $$$

Dining here on dishes made with local
and fresh ingredients is just as magical
as the restaurant's name.

9. American Flatbread

◻ J4 ◻ 137 Maple St, Middlebury
◻ Sun, Mon & L Tue ◻ americanflat
bread.com · $

This wildly popular eatery churns out
gourmet pizzas and salads made with
organic, Vermont-raised ingredients.

10. The Inn at Weathersfield

◻ K5 ◻ 1342 Rte 106, Perkinsville
◻ L, Mon & Tue ◻ weathersfield
inn.com · $$$

Inventive chefs here might pair pork
loin and scallops with capers, or pump-
kin soup with local blue cheese.

NEW HAMPSHIRE

The aptly nicknamed Granite State is a thick wedge of rock between two great rivers – the Connecticut and the Piscataqua. The state itself is carved in half by the great White Mountains. To the north are steep mountain ski runs, snowy peaks beloved by hikers, and seemingly endless hills popular with leaf-peepers in the fall. To the south, broad alpine lakes serve as summer playgrounds for campers and waterskiers. There's an Atlantic coastline here, too; it's short, but still features several swimming beaches. As for big cities, bustling Portsmouth is the place to go for top-notch restaurants, quirky boutiques, and an array of beautiful mansions (which are quintessentially New England in style). The state's capital, Concord, is smaller but still worth seeking out for its historical monuments and quaint local festivals.

1 Top 10 Sights
p121

1 Restaurants
p127

1 The Best of the Rest
p124

1 Pubs and Nightlife
p126

1 Winter Activities
p125

For places to stay in this area, see p151

Waterfront cottages in Portsmouth

1 Portsmouth
⚐ N6

Portsmouth was New Hampshire's first English community, settled at the mouth of the Piscataqua River in 1623. An abundance of timber and a deep harbor made it a natural place for ship-building, and from 1780 to 1870 its merchant traders grew rich. Walk through the handsome squares of the colonial settlement to admire some of New England's finest town mansions, and to breathe the salt air that has always been Portsmouth's lifeblood. The historic houses and period furnishings of Strawbery Banke *(p46)* tell the city's four-centuries-old history.

2 Keene
⚐ L6

At 132-ft- (40-m-) wide for most of its length, Keene's attractive Main Street is easily the widest in New England. This shire town has a lively mix of old-time stores and art galleries, as well as the great bars and cafés you'd expect in a college community. At its center stands the pretty United Church of Christ, known as the "White Church" by locals, with its soaring white steeple.

3 Hanover
⚐ L4

It's hardly a bad thing, but Dartmouth College utterly overwhelms Hanover. The town green and the college green are one and the same, and the shopping district clearly favors the tastes of young scholars and their well-heeled parents. But Dartmouth holds many other riches, even for the visitor just passing through. Not least among them are the art treasures of the soaring, multi-level Hood Museum of Art *(p50)*. Hanover also sits on the shores of the Connecticut River and is popular with canoeists. Most recreational programs of the Dartmouth Outing Club *(Ledyard Canoe Club: 603 643 0709)*, including boat rentals, are open to non-students as well.

4 White Mountains

The White Mountains *(p34)* have a special place in US history. When poets, philosophers, and theologians sought inspiration, they made a pilgrimage to these majestic hills to experience the sublime rising peaks and plunging glens. Today, a variety of attractions bring visitors here.

Waves crashing against a beach in New Hampshire

5 Beaches
🔟 N6

New Hampshire's coastline is more rock than sand, with rugged promontories and rock jetties protecting its fishing harbors. It is also punctuated by swaths of coarse sand. Jenness State Beach and Wallis Sands State Beach in Rye, and Hampton's North Beach, have the best-kept facilities and gentlest swimming. Hampton Beach (p60) is most popular.

6 Concord
🔟 M5

The state capital Concord is a serene little town steeped in history. Its handsome 1819 State House is one of the country's oldest. The celebrated Concord stagecoaches that helped to open up the American West were manufactured here; Mark Twain memorably described one as being "like a cradle on wheels." The city's most famous modern resident was schoolteacher Christa McAuliffe (1948–86), who died aboard the *Challenger* space shuttle. Her dedication to science education is honored at the McAuliffe-Shepard Discovery Center (p70).

7 Lake Sunapee
🔟 L5

This alpine lake – whose name, meaning "wild goose waters," is of Algonkian origin – was a Victorian resort where vacationers stepped off the train onto steamboats to be delivered to their grand lakefront hotels. The hotels are gone, but private cottages ring the lake, and the harbors of Sunapee and Newbury are busy spots in the summer, with free outdoor concerts and bustling restaurants. Take a scenic cruise on the lake, or enjoy a dinner cruise with Sunapee Cruises (sunapeecruises.com).

8 Lakes Region
🔟

Vast lakes and small ponds form a stunning watery belt (p36) across New Hampshire's midriff. Seek solitude among the loons on a remote cove, or party all night on Weirs Beach.

9 Yankee Country
🔟 L6

Yankee Publishing, which produces both *Yankee Magazine* and the *Old*

LIVE FREE OR DIE

Some visitors might imagine that the state motto proclaimed on license plates refers to New Hampshire's lack of sales and income taxes. In fact it originated with a toast that the state's Revolutionary War soldier, General John Stark, gave by letter to the 1809 reunion of veterans of the Battle of Bennington, when poor health pre-vented him from attending: "Live free or die: death is not the worst of evils."

Farmer's Almanac, is based in Dublin. The homespun village and its neighboring towns of Peterborough and Jaffrey epitomize the gentle Yankee Country. The region was a popular resort area in the late 19th century, and all three villages have long served as staging grounds for people preparing to climb the nearby Mount Monadnock (*p63*), said to be the second-most-climbed peak in the world after Japan's Mount Fuji.

10 Manchester
🅟 M6

The largest city in northern New England, Manchester rose and fell with the Amoskeag Mill. From humble beginnings in 1809 on the east bank of the Merrimack River, the town grew into the world's largest cotton-mill complex by the dawn of the 20th century. The textile era has long since ended here, but the hulking brick mills have been transformed into a complex of restaurants, college classrooms, offices, and apartments. The city's comprehensive Currier Museum of Art (*p48*) is the state's premier art museum, promising paintings, photographs, and sculpture.

Exploring Manchester's Currier Museum of Art

A DAY'S DRIVE ON THE KANCAMAGUS HIGHWAY

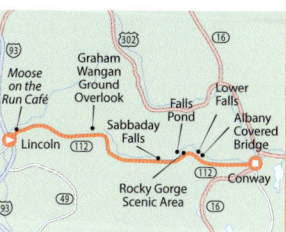

Morning

Before you begin the 35-mile (56-km) drive from **Lincoln** to **Conway** (*p34*), stop at **Moose on the Run Café** (*mooseonthe runcafe.com*) for picnic fixings. After a gentle 11-mile (18-km) rise, you'll climb through steep switchbacks for 4 miles (6 km) to the **Graham Wangan Ground Overlook**. As the road twists and turns, watch for the trailhead to **Sabbaday Falls**. A short walk through dense, pine-scented woods brings you to the waterfall, which makes a wonderfully dramatic 90-degree dogleg as it tumbles down. The **Rocky Gorge Scenic Area**, a further 4 miles (6 km) east, is a geological wonder. Cross a bridge to **Falls Pond**, where anglers cast for trout.

Afternoon

Another 3 miles (5 km) east, picnic at **Lower Falls**, overlooking the boulder-strewn Swift River. The green pools below the largest boulders make cool summer swimming holes. In the fall, photographers scramble trying to capture the intense red and yellow foliage. From the falls, drive to the **Albany Covered Bridge**. The weathered 120-ft (37-m) span is a favorite with photographers. From the bridge, it's about 7 flat miles (11 km) to the end of the "Kanc" in Conway.

The Best of the Rest

M-26 Pershing tanks in the Wright Museum

1. Children's Museum of New Hampshire
N5 6 Washington St, Dover 9am–noon & 1–4pm Tue–Sat; 9am–noon Sun childrens-museum.org

Fascinating exhibits on a range of topics, from submarines to world culture, make this museum the perfect place for kids.

2. Mount Kearsarge Indian Museum
L5 18 Highlawn Rd, Warner May–Oct: daily indianmuseum.org

Admire intricate craftwork and learn about the Indigenous peoples' connection with nature at this museum.

3. Mount Sunapee State Park
L5 86 Beach Access Rd, Newbury Late May–mid-Sep nhstateparks.org

Skiing in winter and swimming, fishing, and boating in summer, make this state park ideal for outdoor activities.

4. Enfield Shaker Museum
L5 447 Rte 4A, Enfield Jun–Oct shakermuseum.org

This informative museum is dedicated to preserving the Shakers' heritage, with exhibits and artifacts that chronicle their lives here.

5. Odiorne Point State Park
N6 Rte 1A, Rye nhstateparks.org

Located in the town of Rye, this park includes the US military's Fort Dearborn and a science center, along with fishing, hiking, and cycling facilities.

6. Wright Museum
M5 77 Center St, Wolfeboro 10am–4pm Mon–Sat, noon–4pm Sun wrightmuseum.org

From the military to pop culture and civilian life, this museum captures the nation's sentiment during World War II.

7. Wellington State Park
L5 614 W. Shore Rd, Bristol nhstateparks.org

Wellington State Park prides itself on being the largest freshwater swimming beach in the state. Its hiking trails lead to the summits of the Little and Big Sugarloaf mountains.

8. Crawford Notch State Park
M4 1464 Rte 302, Hart's Location nhstateparks.org

The vast wilderness of Crawford Notch State Park is a hiker's paradise. Climb Mount Willard for superb views.

9. Budweiser Brewery Experience
M6 221 Daniel Webster Hwy, Merrimack Hours vary, check website budweisertours.com

Beer lovers can learn more about this brewery's history, as well as the art of brewing, through tours that also include free tastings.

10. Rhododendron State Park
L6 424 Rockwood Pond Rd, Fitzwilliam nhstateparks.org

Named for the vibrant pink and red rhododendrons that bloom around mid-July, this park is also famed for its berries, laurel, and heathers.

Winter Activities

1. UNH Wildcats Hockey

N5 Whittemore Center, 128 Main St, Durham Oct–Apr unhwildcats.com

A cheerful, family-friendly atmosphere underscores the games of this powerhouse college Division I hockey team.

2. Outdoor Skating

M4 Schouler Park, Main St, North Conway Dec–Mar

Schouler Park in North Conway offers a great experience for both beginner and advanced skaters, weather permitting.

3. Nordic Skiing

M4

Enjoy cross-country skiing at the Nordic Center, which offers scenic trails along the majestic White Mountain National Forest. The Waterville Valley Resort (waterville.com) also provides exciting skiing opportunities.

4. SnowCoach

M3 Great Glen Trails, 1 Mt. Washington Auto Rd, Gorham Dec–Mar: daily mt-washington.com

This special van transports visitors to the treeline at a height of 4,200 ft (1,280 m), on the Mount Washington Auto Road, offering superb winter views.

5. Snow Tubing

M3 Great Glen Trails, 1 Mt. Washington Auto Rd, Gorham Dec–Mar: daily greatglentrails.com

A fun-filled family adventure, snow tubing involves zipping down a hill on a cushy inner tube.

6. Ice Climbing

M4

Learn to climb in ice and snow with crampons, picks, ropes, and harnesses on Mount Washington. Adventure outfitters Eastern Mountain School (emsoutdoors.com) provide specialized gear.

7. Snowshoeing

M5

Snowshoeing involves walking on snow wearing specialized snowshoes. Prescott Farm (prescottfarm.org) has over 3 miles (5 km) of woodland, pond, and field trails for snowshoeing. Modest fee for snowshoe rental.

8. Snowmobiling

L4

Marvel at the hushed beauty of New Hampshire's snow-clad mountains in winter on a guided snowmobile tour from Sled Ventures snowmobile rentals (nhsledadventures.com).

9. Alpine Skiing

L/M 3–4

Thanks to the White Mountains, New Hampshire has a multitude of top-class alpine ski runs and all are easily reached via Rte 16 or 1-91.

10. New England Ski Museum

L3 Exit 34B I-93/Franconia Notch Parkway, Franconia Late May–Mar: daily skimuseum.org

The first aerial ski tramway in the US opened on Cannon Mountain in 1938. This is, therefore, a fitting location for this ski museum that traces the development of the sport from its roots to more modern times.

**Ice climbing on the slopes
of the White Mountains**

Live performance at Irish pub, The Shaskeen

Pubs and Nightlife

1. Elm City Brewing
📍 L6 🏠 Colony Mill Marketplace, 222 West St, Keene 🌐 elmcitybrewing.com
Famous for its four-beer samplers, Elm City Brewing offers a taste of local ales, porters, and stouts. Its cozy booths make it the ideal spot for conversation.

2. Harlow's Pub
📍 L6 🏠 3 School St, Peterborough 🌐 harlowspub.com
Visit this relaxed venue on Thursday nights for a bluegrass jam; or try weekends, when it might be rock and blues, reggae, or jazz.

3. Strange Brew Tavern
📍 M6 🏠 88 Market St, Manchester 🌐 strangebrewtavern.net
This bustling tavern serves a wide range of local brews along with an extensive menu of familiar pub grub. Local bands perform most nights.

4. The Press Room
📍 N6 🏠 77 Daniel St, Portsmouth 🌐 pressroomnh.com
Established in 1976, this pub features live jazz. The rest of the week might bring Celtic music and sea shanties, blues, soul, folk, or even poetry.

5. Flying Goose Brew Pub
📍 L5 🏠 40 Andover Rd, New London 🌐 flyinggoose.com
With a schedule of live music, "the Goose" lures regulars and travelers alike for hearty traditional food, malty ales made on the premises, and lively conversation.

6. The Shaskeen
📍 M6 🏠 909 Elm St, Manchester 🌐 shasheenirishpub.com
Established by two Irish musicians, this atmospheric pub offers equally stellar food and music.

7. Patrick's Pub and Eatery
📍 M5 🏠 18 Weirs Rd, Gilford 🌐 patrichspub.com
Trivia nights, open-mic nights, and Saturday musical sessions, plus plenty of pints of Guinness, create a lively atmosphere at Patrick's.

8. Barley House
📍 M5 🏠 132 N Main St, Concord 🌐 thebarleyhouse.com
A local favorite, The Barley is well known for its tavern fare, craft beers, and cocktails.

9. Woodstock Inn Station and Brewery
📍 L4 🏠 135 Main St, North Woodstock 🌐 woodstochinnbrewery.com
English malts and international hops yield a range of outstanding ales geared for outdoors enthusiasts.

10. Moat Mountain Smoke House and Brewing Co
📍 M4 🏠 3378 White Mountain Hwy, Rte 16, North Conway 🌐 moatmountain.com
This ski-country restaurant takes BBQ seriously. The brisket is Texas dry rub, the pork comes Carolina-style (vinegar doused), with St. Louis-style ribs. Match them all with the caramel brown ale.

Restaurants

PRICE CATEGORIES

For a three-course meal for one with half a bottle of wine (or equivalent meal), taxes and extra charges.

....

$ under $45 **$$** $45–$80 **$$$** over $80

---

1. Ristorante Massimo

N6 59 Penhallow St, Portsmouth L ristorantemassimo.com · **$$**

Sophisticated, largely northern Italian dishes make great use of New England seafood, especially lobster. The romantic dining room in the restaurant is set in a Federal-era custom house.

2. Black Trumpet Bistro

N6 29 Ceres St, Portsmouth L, Mon blacktrumpetbistro.com · **$$**

Located alongside the harbor, this bistro and bar has cozy interiors and excellent food.

3. The Restaurant at Burdick's

K6 47 Main St, Walpole Mon, D Tue & Sun 47main walpole.com · **$$**

Casual country French dining at this bistro complements the artisanal chocolates sold in the adjoining room.

4. Cotton

M6 75 Arms St, Manchester L, Sun & Mon cottonfood.com · **$$**

Start with New Hampshire's best martini, then order from the menu of updated comfort-food – meatloaf and mash, steak salad, buttermilk-fried chicken – in this uber-hip spot.

5. Sole's

L6 8 Winter St, Keene 716-551-0983 L, Sun & Mon · **$$**

This speakeasy-style restaurant offers excellent cocktails and a great menu of comfort-food classics, including chicken burgers and meatloaf. The staff serves guests while dressed in 1920s period costumes.

6. Hart's Turkey Farm Restaurant

M5 233 Daniel Webster Hwy, Rtes 3 & 104, Meredith hartsturkey farm.com · **$**

It's Thanksgiving every day at this family restaurant specializing in roast turkey dinners with all the trimmings.

7. Pine

L4 2 S Main St, Hanover 603 646 8000 · **$$**

A venerable inn, Pine serves as the center of Dartmouth College's social scene. It offers farm-to-table fare.

8. Three Chimneys Inn

N6 17 Newmarket Rd, Durham L, Sun–Tue threechimneys inn.com · **$$**

With a focus on farm-to-table dining, this inn uses local produce to highlight the taste of New Hampshire cuisine.

9. The Grazing Room

L5 3 The Oaks, Henniker L, Mon & Tue colbyhillinn.com · **$$**

Located in a romantic country setting, Colby Hill offers stately dining on classic New England dishes.

10. Ariana's Restaurant

L4 1 Market St, Lyme L, Mon–Wed arianasrestaurant.com · **$$**

An outstanding farm-to-fork restaurant, Ariana serves excellent American fare with Italian flavors.

Pine's cozy, wood-paneled interior

MAINE

Larger than New Hampshire, Connecticut, Rhode Island, and Vermont combined, Maine is New England on a magnificent scale. With a coast that meanders around peninsulas and flows into harbors for an astonishing 5,500 miles (8,850 km) between Kittery and Calais, the state promises plenty to see without abandoning the smell of salt air. Turn off Route 1 down any peninsula, and you enter a world of breathtaking vistas and small villages, with a lobster harbor at the tip; beaches, meanwhile, stretch for miles along Maine's south coast. A province of Massachusetts from 1652 to 1820, Maine was famous well into the 20th century for harvesting timber and building tall ships. Even today, the state's windjammer fleet is one of the world's largest.

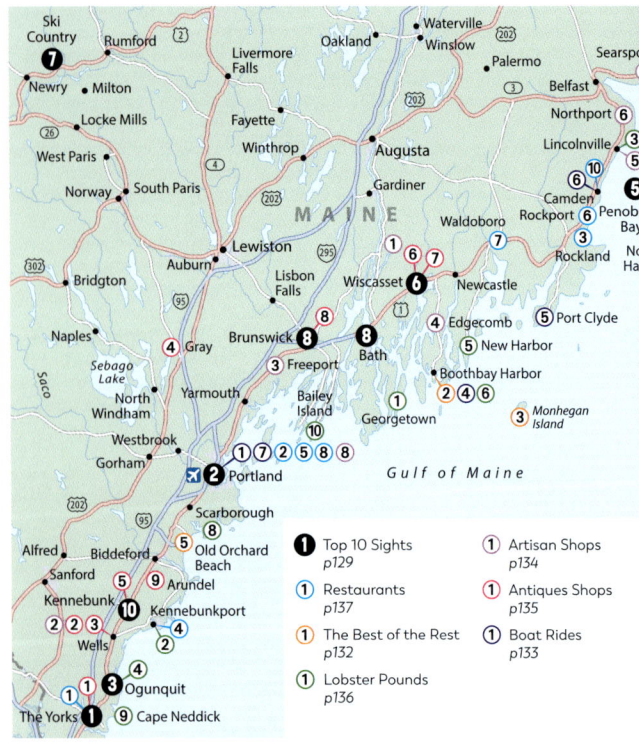

- ❶ Top 10 Sights *p129*
- ① Restaurants *p137*
- ① The Best of the Rest *p132*
- ① Lobster Pounds *p136*
- ① Artisan Shops *p134*
- ① Antiques Shops *p135*
- ① Boat Rides *p133*

For places to stay in this area, see p151

Nubble lighthouse overlooking the Atlantic Ocean, The Yorks

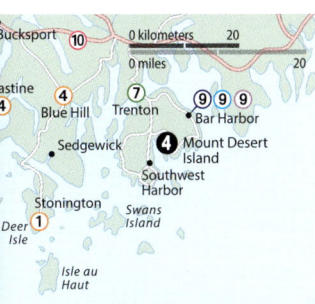

Northern Maine

1 The Yorks
☑ N5 & N6

York has two very different faces: the historical York Village and the brassy summer playground of York Beach. Maine's first successful European settlement, York was founded in 1634; the Old York Historical Society *(oldyork.org)* chronicles local history. Long Sands and Short Sands swimming beaches are the main draws at York Beach, which is also good for surfing and has an arcade. Drive to the end of Cape Neddick to see the iconic Nubble Light.

2 Portland and Casco Bay

Maine's largest community has the cultural advantages of a mid-sized city *(p32)* and all the natural beauty of a handsome, well-protected bay. The once-bedraggled maritime area has been reborn in the animated Old Port.

3 Ogunquit
☑ N5

Plein air painters found Ogunquit in the 1890s, and visitors have been seeing beauty at every turn since. The picturesque Perkins Cove bristles with art galleries, souvenir stores, and seafood shacks. Marginal Way, a short trail north of the cove, is lined with beach roses.

Stunning view of Jordan Pond, Mount Desert Island

4 Mount Desert Island
French explorer Samuel de Champlain pinned the name *Ile des Monts Deserts* on this large island (*p30*) in 1604, and the name "island of bare mountains" has stuck. The rocky balds that Champlain observed are prized among hikers and climbers in Acadia National Park.

5 Penobscot Bay
Q3
The west coast of Penobscot Bay is Maine's best-kept secret, although most of the state's windjammers anchor in Rockland and Camden. Rockland is Maine's lobster capital and home of the treasured Farnsworth Art Museum (*p53*); Camden has a beautiful harbor – a yacht-filled silver bowl at the foot of a mountain; Belfast is a community where artisans set the tone.

6 Wiscasset
P4
Even simply driving through, you'll have plenty of time to contemplate Wiscasset's self-description as "the prettiest village in Maine" because the narrow bridge across the Sheepscot River backs traffic up in midsummer. Better to park and walk around this stunning village where adept 18th- and 19th-century shipwrights turned their talents to building houses for sea captains.

7 Ski Country
N2
Moist air masses sweeping up the eastern seaboard meet the icy jet stream bringing Arctic air off the Canadian shield in northwest Maine, just east of the White Mountains. The result is massive dumps of snow that guarantee the peaks around Bethel, Newry, Kingfield, and Jackman will be buried in the white gold that skiers crave. In the summertime, long green meadows are transformed into championship golf courses.

8 Bath and Brunswick
P4
Nearly half the US ocean-going sailing vessels launched in the late 19th century went down the ways from Bath shipyards – a history detailed at the Maine Maritime Museum (*p55*). This ship-building ability earned it the nickname, "the city of ships." Nearby, Brunswick is better known for making scholars than ships. Bowdoin College educated authors Nathaniel Hawthorne and Henry Wadsworth Longfellow, as well as intrepid Arctic explorers Robert Peary and Donald MacMillan. The college's Peary-MacMillan Arctic Museum (*p50*) displays artifacts and images from their expeditions.

THE MAINE MOOSE

The official state animal, the moose (*Alces alces*) is found all over Maine, with the greatest concentrations near Moosehead and Rangeley lakes. They often cross roads at dawn and dusk, so take special care while driving through swampy areas. An 800-lb (363-kg) gentle giant makes a considerable impact in a collision.

9 Moosehead Lake

P1 480 Moosehead Lake Rd, Greenville destinationmooseheadlake.com

The largest body of water contained within a single New England state, this lake resembles the antlers of a moose from above, and if you take a seaplane tour, you'll almost certainly see some of these impressive animals out for a swim. The lake is known for hunting, fishing, and winter snowmobiling, but photographic moose safaris are increasingly popular. Inquire about them at Greenville's visitor center.

10 Kennebunk

N5

The town of Kennebunk developed two distinct villages: Kennebunk on the river, and Kennebunkport where the river meets the ocean. Once a ship-building center, Kennebunk has now become principally a community of summer vacation homes. Visit the Brick Store Museum (brickstoremuseum.org) for exhibits on the town's cultural and historic heritage, and the exquisite Wedding Cake House (weddingcakehouse.com) to marvel at its intricate workmanship. Then head to Dock Square in Kennebunkport to peruse the boutiques, galleries, souvenir stores, and a number of bed and breakfasts. It's one of the most affluent communities in the state.

Upscale houses in the town of Kennebunkport

A DAY'S DRIVE IN WYETH COUNTRY

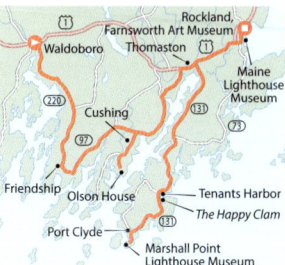

Morning

The rocky Maine coast has entranced many painters, but Andrew Wyeth (1917–2009) was among the few to chart the quiet country life of the saltwater farms.

This drive shows you Maine through Wyeth's eyes. From Rte 1 in **Waldoboro**, turn south toward the village of **Friendship**, famed for its namesake sloop. Continue north toward **Cushing**. The **Olson House** was made famous in Wyeth's *Christina's World* (1948), and it looks the same since Wyeth painted it. Carry on north to Rte 1, passing through handsome **Thomaston**, and turn right at High St (Rte 131). Enjoy stunning vistas as you drive to **Port Clyde**, where the Monhegan Island (p132) ferry departs.

Afternoon

North of the harbor, look for signs to the **Marshall Point Lighthouse Museum**. The light was automated in 1971; the former keeper's house is a local history museum (p59). Head north toward **Tenants Harbor** for an early lobster dinner at **The Happy Clam** (River Rd). Continue north to Rockland, to visit the **Maine Lighthouse Museum** (p55), and spend time at the **Farnsworth Art Museum** (p53) enjoying works by Wyeth and Louise Nevelson.

The Best of the Rest

1. Deer Isle and Stonington
Q3

Art and fishing seem to come together in Maine. The Haystack Mountain School of Crafts made Deer Isle renowned years ago, while the lobster boats still outnumber pleasure crafts in the harbor at Stonington.

2. Boothbay Harbor
P4

The boating capital of midcoast Maine, this picturesque harbor is a great spot to go on a whale-watching trip, kayak excursion, or pleasure cruise.

3. Monhegan Island
Q4

Birders and hikers flock to the rocky cliffs of this offshore art colony in summer. After peak season, the lobster industry prepares for the winter catch.

4. Castine and Blue Hill
Q3 & R3

A drive down a single peninsula takes you to two great towns: art-minded Blue Hill, with its excellent pottery studios; and Castine, with its rich colonial heritage.

5. Old Orchard Beach
N5

A sandy beach with gentle surf, the Old Orchard Beach is the perfect place for swimming. Kids love the amusement park rides, the waterslide, and the pier with its fast-food vendors and games of skill.

6. Campobello Island
R2 visitmaine.com

Visitors can drive from the little town of Lubec over a bridge to Campobello Island, which is part of Canada. Franklin Roosevelt frequently summered on this scenic island and his house is now a museum (*rooseveltcampobello.org*).

7. Bangor
Q2

Fine mansions dot this Penobscot River town, once the world's timber capital, and today, a starting point to the northern wilderness.

8. Baxter State Park
Y5 64 Balsam Dr, Millinocket; baxterstateparkauthority.com

Test your physical mettle by scaling 5,267-ft (1,605-m) Mount Katahdin, set inside 327 sq miles (848 sq km) of pristine forest.

9. Rangeley Lake Region
N2

Spruce- and hemlock-clad peaks rise with robust grace from a plateau splashed with 112 lakes and ponds – an outdoors enthusiast's paradise. Birders can visit the Perham Birding Trail to look for the resident and migratory birds.

10. Allagash Wilderness
Y4–Y5 18 Elkins Ln, Augusta; 207 287 3821

Forever wild, the Allagash is a legendary system of rivers and lakes where the trout (and the mosquitoes) are bigger than anywhere else.

Hiking through Baxter State Park, Maine

Boat Rides

1. Casco Bay Lines
📍 N4 🏠 56 Commercial St, Portland
🌐 cascobaylines.com 🔗

The oldest ferry service in the US, Casco Bay Lines runs passenger and freight ferries all through the year. Its services also include sunrise, sunset, and moonlight cruises.

2. Three Rivers Whitewater
📍 P1 🏠 2265 Rte 201, West Forhs
🕐 May–Oct 🌐 threeriverswhitewater.com 🔗

Guides negotiate the thrilling waves and rapids on this rafting trip down the Kennebec River in Maine.

3. Bold Coast Charter Company
📍 R2 🏠 Cutler Harbor 🕐 May–mid-Aug 🌐 boldcoast.com 🔗

About 10,000 endangered puffins nest on Machias Seal Island. Bold Coast offers sightseeing trips for bird-watchers and photographers.

4. Cap'n Fish's Whale Watch
📍 P4 🏠 1 Wharf St, Boothbay Harbor 🕐 Late May–mid-Oct
🌐 boothbayboattrips.com 🔗

Go whale-watching with the help of a shipboard naturalist along the scenic Maine coast. You might spot seals, porpoises, and dolphins, too.

5. Monhegan Boat Line
📍 Q4 🏠 Port Clyde 🌐 monheganboat.com 🔗

Drift past lobster boats on the trip out from Port Clyde to Monhegan Island, or opt for a cruise. The ferry operates year-round, while cruises are available from June to August.

6. Schooner Appledore
📍 Q3 🏠 Bayview Landing, Camden 🕐 Jun–Oct 🌐 appledore2.com 🔗

Enjoy sailing tours on the famous Maine windjammers around the Penobscot Bay. Private sailing charters are also available.

Sunset cruise aboard Schooner *Appledore II*

7. Portland Schooner Co.
📍 N4 🏠 Maine State Pier, Portland
🕐 Mid-May–Oct 🌐 portlandschooner.com 🔗

Three historic schooners make two-hour sails through the waters of Casco Bay. Spot seals and seabirds, and enjoy nonstop views of the rugged coastline.

8. SS Katahdin
📍 P1 🏠 12 Lily Bay Rd, Greenville
🕐 Late Jun–mid-Oct 🌐 katahdincruises.com 🔗

Moosehead Lake is stunning during the fall foliage and there can be no better way to survey the scene than aboard the gloriously preserved SS *Katahdin*, a 1914 steamboat that was built in the city of Bath in Maine.

9. Downeast Windjammer Cruises
📍 R3 🏠 Bar Harbor Inn Pier, Bar Harbor 🕐 May–Oct 🌐 downeastwindjammer.com 🔗

Visitors can enjoy stunning vistas of Frenchman Bay aboard historic schooners and a lobster sloop, which offer day sails around the islands.

10. Allagash Canoe Trips
📍 Y5 🏠 Greenville 🕐 May–Sep
🌐 allagashcanoetrips.com 🔗

The Allagash River and Chamberlain Lake offer paddling journeys in the North Woods wilderness and excellent avenues for trout fishing as well.

Artisan Shops

Indigenous Wabanaki artifacts at the Abbe Museum

1. Tandem Glass

🏆 P3 📍 6 Eagle Lodge Ln, Dresden
🌐 tandemglass.com

Terrill Waldman and Charlie Jenkins have crafted attractive hand-blown art glass since 2006, at their saltbox barn studio and gallery.

2. Weathervanes of Maine

🏆 N5 📍 1451 Rte 1, Wells
🌐 weathervanesofmaine.com

Weathervanes once topped every Maine barn. This company helps keep the tradition alive, with its menagerie of hand-crafted copper animals.

3. Thos. Moser Cabinetmakers

🏆 P4 📍 149 Main St, Freeport
🌐 thosmoser.com

You might pick up some home decorating tips in this restored 19th-century home, where modern paintings and photography are displayed next to the cabinetmakers' furniture.

4. Edgecomb Potters Gallery and Studio Complex

🏆 P4 📍 727 Boothbay Rd, Rte 27S, Edgecomb 📞 207 882 9493

Richly colored glazes are the hallmark of Edgecomb porcelain, which is on sale here alongside pieces by other artisans, working in wood, metal, and glass.

5. Maine Artisans

🏆 Q3 📍 2518 Atlantic Hwy, Lincolnville Beach 🌐 maine artisanscollective.com

Representing the creativity of mid-coast Maine, this cooperative gallery sells knitted socks and driftwood lamps, delicate glass orchids, and paintings on slate, among other wares.

6. Swans Island Company

🏆 Q3 📍 231 Rte 1, Northport
🌐 swansislandcompany.com

An elegant pure-wool Swans Island blanket is the ultimate word in cold-weather luxury. The Northport showroom-studio is set in a lovely converted 1780s farmhouse.

7. Bluejacket Ship Crafters

🏆 Q3 📍 160 E Main St, Searsport
🌐 bluejacketinc.com

The oldest ship-modeling company in US, Bluejacket has over 100 examples on display. Select a kit for a sailing sloop, or radio-controlled lobster boat.

8. Maine Potters Market

🏆 N4 📍 376 Fore St, Portland
🌐 mainepottersmarket.com

Representing 14 potters around the state, this shop reflects the diverse styles and visions of Maine artists working with clay.

9. Abbe Museum

🏆 R3 📍 26 Mount Desert St, Rte 3, Bar Harbor 🌐 abbemuseum.org

This museum gift store has prized sweetgrass, ash, and birchbark baskets made by Maine's Wabanaki peoples.

10. Columbia Falls Pottery

🏆 R2 📍 4 Main St, Machias
🌐 columbiafallspottery.com

This pottery shop offers tiles, clocks, lamps, and crocks – each piece is hand-painted with charming local motifs, including blueberries, sailboats, lupines, and shorebirds.

Antiques Shops

1. York Antiques Gallery
N5 | 746 Rte 1, York
W yorkantiques.com
Dealers at this gallery specialize in fine 18th- and 19th-century furniture and accessories. You probably won't find a bargain, but you might pick up decorating ideas.

2. Bo-Mar Antiques and Collectibles
N5 | 1626 Post Rd, Wells
One of the largest group shops on the Maine coast, Bo-Mar booths offer a huge range of items, including sports collectibles, jewelry, glass, porcelain, linens, and kitchen tools.

3. Douglas N. Harding Rare Books
N5 | 1885 Post Rd, Wells
You'll find volumes on everything from circus arts to UFOs in this 14-room store with over 100,000 used and rare books.

4. Barn on 26 Antiques
N4 | 361 Shaker Rd, Gray
W barnon26.com
This 1870 barn is set on a scenic country road between Portland and the Sebago Lake. It is filled with an assortment of furniture and furnishings dating from between the Civil War and World War I.

5. The Old House Parts Co.
N5 | 1 Trackside Dr, Kennebunk
W oldhouseparts.com
As the name suggests, this store deals in antique architectural pieces and old hardware. It has an expansive inventory, featuring vintage mantels, light fixtures, and old machine parts.

6. Pumpkin Patch Antiques
Q3 | 15 Rte 1, Searsport
W dennisraleighantiques.com
This shop sells mid-20th-century quilts, nautical items, and porcelain that reflect Searsport's maritime history.

7. Wiscasset Antiques Center, Wiscasset
P4 | 4 Hodge St, Wiscasset
W wiscassetantiquescenter.com
This friendly store features a collection of American Revolution-era antiques, ranging from centuries-old guns to historic swords.

8. Cabot Mill Antiques
P4 | 14 Maine St, Brunswick
W cabotiques.com
This restored brick textile mill is home to 160 booths that sell a variety of folk art, nautical antiques, period furniture, art, pottery, and vintage jewelry. It's one of the largest multi-dealer stores in the area.

9. Antiques USA
N5 | Rte 1, Arundel
W antiquesusamaine.com
Route 1 from York to Arundel is dense with antiques stores. Antiques USA is one of the largest, bringing hundreds of dealers with different tastes and interests under one roof. It's well worth seeking out.

10. Big Chicken Barn Books and Antiques
R3 | 1768 Buchsport Rd, Ellsworth
W bigchickenbarn.com
The owners of this gigantic emporium encourage browsers to bring a picnic lunch. It takes hours to peruse the thousands of magazines, rare books, and antiques.

Goods for sale at Cabot Mill Antiques

Lobster Pounds

1. Five Islands Lobster Co.
P4 1447 Five Islands Rd, Georgetown Mid-Oct–early May fiveislandslobster.com • $
Lobstermen stream in all day as diners crack lobsters, dip the meat in melted butter, and enjoy stunning views.

2. The Clam Shack
N5 On the Bridge, Kennebunkport Mid-Oct–mid-May theclamshack.net • $
The namesake fried clams are always good, but the real specialty here is the lobster roll.

3. The Lobster Pound
Q3 2521 Rte 1, Lincolnville Beach Mid-Oct–mid-May lobsterpoundmaine.com • $
Take a dip, then savor a boiled lobster dinner – or dine inside to escape the mendicant gulls.

4. Barnacle Billy's
N5 70 Perkins Cove Rd, Ogunquit Nov–mid-Apr barnbilly.com • $
A bargain-hunter's choice in a pricey resort, Billy's has a full-service restaurant and a bare-bones seafood shack.

5. Cook's Lobster and Ale House
P4 68 Garrison Cove Rd, Bailey Island Mon & Tue cookslobster.com • $
Enjoy your lobster surrounded on three sides by water, with a view of the world's only crib-stone bridge.

Boats moored near Barnacle Billy's in Perkins Cove

Maine's classic lobster roll

6. Boothbay Lobster Wharf
P4 97 Atlantic Ave, Boothbay Harbor Mid-Oct–mid-May boothbaylobsterwharf.com • $$
In a legendary lobstering harbor, the Lobster Wharf has the shortest possible distance from trap to plate.

7. Trenton Bridge Lobster Pound
R3 1237 Bar Harbor Rd, Trenton Mid-Oct–late Apr trentonbridge lobster.com • $
All you need are lobster, nutcrackers, picks, and plenty of napkins at this pound, located on the mainland side from Mount Desert Island.

8. Bayley's Lobster Pound
N5 9 Ave 6, Pine Point, Scarborough Mid-Oct–late Apr bayleys.com • $
Founded in 1915, there are some great specialties offered here, like lobster-stuffed mushrooms and crabcakes.

9. Cape Neddick Lobster Pound
N5 60 Shore Rd, Cape Neddich Hours vary, chech website cape neddichlobsterpound.com • $$
Sample the steamed mussels or clams first, before cracking into the main attraction on the menu.

10. Shaw's Fish and Lobster Wharf
P4 129 Rte 32, New Harbor Mid-Oct–mid-May shaws-wharf.com • $
A lobster lover's paradise, Shaw's has great views of the harbor, a raw bar, and a full liquor license.

Restaurants

PRICE CATEGORIES

For a three-course meal for one with half a bottle of wine (or equivalent meal), taxes and extra charges.

$ under $45 $$ $45–$85 $$$ over $85

1. Dockside

N6 22 Harris Island Rd, York
Nov–May docksidegq.com · $$

An island location in York Harbor, Dockside is popular for its fish dishes, from fresh haddock to diver scallops and clams from nearby beds. Cioppino of Maine seafood is always a good bet.

2. Eventide Oyster Co.

N4 86 Middle St, Portland
eventideoysterco.com · $$

Favored by hipsters, this restaurant serves an array of fresh oysters and other local delicacies of the sea.

3. Primo Restaurant

Q3 2 S Main St, Rochland
L, Mon &Tue primorestaur ant.com · $$$

The chef here conjures up culinary wonders from mostly home-grown produce – even Brussels sprouts get to be stars in season.

4. White Barn Inn

N5 37 Beach Ave, Kennebunkport
L aubergeresorts.com/whitebarn inn · $$$

Two 1820s barns make a surprisingly elegant and restful space in which to enjoy the four-course prix-fixe menu.

5. Chaval

N4 58 Pine St, Portland
L & Sun chavalmaine.com · $$

This West End brasserie offers an American menu with French and Spanish accents.

6. Nina June

Q3 24 Central St, Rochport
Sun–Tue ninajunerestaurant. com · $$$

A Mediterranean-style restaurant overlooking picturesque Rockport harbor, Nina June is known for its classic Maine dishes.

7. Moody's Diner

Q3 1885 Rte 1, Waldoboro
moodysdiner.com · $

Vacationers and Mainers rub elbows in this iconic diner. Try the blueberry muffins, or the turkey dinner followed by walnut pie.

8. Fore Street

N4 288 Fore St, Portland L
forestreet.biz · $$$

Sample the wildly popular wood-oven roasted mussels from a menu built largely around local ingredients.

9. West Street Cafe

R3 76 West St, Bar Harbor
Nov–Apr weststreetcafe.com · $$

Bright and casual, West Street is known for the classic trio of corn, lobster, and blueberry pie.

10. Natalie's

Q3 Camden Harbour Inn, 83 Bay View St, Camden L cam denharbourinn.com/natalies- restaurant · $$$

Penobscot Bay seafood and local produce underpin the elegant con- temporary regional cooking here.

Raw bar at the Eventide Oyster Co.

STREETSMART

Winding through the woods, Vermont

GETTING AROUND

Whether you're visiting New England for a weekend break or a week-long road-trip, discover how best to reach your destination and travel around like a pro.

PUBLIC TRANSPORTATION

BOSTON
$2.40
One-way subway fare

PORTLAND
$2.50
Single local bus journey

PROVIDENCE
$2.00
Single local bus journey

SPEED LIMITS

INTERSTATE HIGHWAYS
65 mph
(105 km/h)

MAJOR HIGHWAYS
55 mph
(95 km/h)

TOWN CENTERS
30 mph
(45 km/h)

URBAN ZONES
25 mph
(40 km/h)

Arriving by Air

Logan International Airport in Boston is the principal gateway airport to New England, located only 3 miles (5 km) from downtown Boston. The cheapest and quickest method to make your way into the city from the airport is via the free **MBTA** Silver Line buses that run to South Station in downtown Boston. These are accessible for people with specific requirements.

A few international flights also arrive at Connecticut's **Bradley International Airport**. Meanwhile, **T. F. Green Airport** in Providence, Rhode Island, and **Manchester-Boston Regional Airport** in New Hampshire are served by a handful of domestic carriers.

Bradley International Airport (BDL)
W bradleyairport.com
Logan International Airport (BOS)
W massport.com
Manchester-Boston Regional Airport (MHT)
W flymanchester.com
MBTA
W mbta.com
T. F. Green Airport (PVD)
W flyri.com

Rail Travel

Amtrak trains from New York follow three main routes in New England. The Northeast Regional route covers Long Island Sound, Connecticut, and Providence, and continues to Boston's South Station. The Vermonter follows the Connecticut River, while the Ethan Allen takes the eastern banks of Lake Champlain to Burlington, Vermont. Amtrak's Downeaster service leaves Boston's North Station, with stops in New Hampshire and Maine, and ending in Brunswick, Maine.

Amtrak
W amtrak.com

Bus Travel

Concord Coach Lines serves Maine and New Hampshire. **Peter Pan** has stops in

Connecticut, Rhode Island, and western Massachusetts. Other parts of Massachusetts, such as Cape Cod and the South Shore, are served by **Plymouth & Brockton**. FlixBus runs from Boston to New Haven and New York. **Megabus** serves Portland, Boston, and New York.

Concord Coach Lines
W concordcoachlines.com

FlixBus
W flixbus.com

Megabus
W megabus.com

Peter Pan
W peterpanbus.com

Plymouth & Brockton
W p-b.com

Boats and Ferries
The CAT high-speed car ferry connects Bar Harbor, Maine, and Yarmouth, Nova Scotia, in about 3.5 hours, from spring to fall. The **Steamship Authority** and **Hy-Line Cruises** depart Hyannis and Woods Hole, Massachusetts, for Nantucket and Martha's Vineyard islands.

The CAT
W ferries.ca/thecat

Hy-Line Cruises
W hylinecruises.com

Steamship Authority
W steamshipauthority.com

Public Transportation
Very little public transportation in New England is integrated between regions. **RIPTA** (Rhode Island Public Transit Authority) operates an extensive bus service throughout Rhode Island, with special beach buses from urban centers in the summer. The MBTA (Massachusetts Bay Transportation Authority) operates the subway (known more commonly as the "T") and bus lines in the Metropolitan Boston area, as well as commuter trains running north to Newburyport, west to Worcester, and south to Providence, Rhode Island. Safety and hygiene measures, timetables, ticket information, transport maps,

and more can be obtained from the websites of individual operators.

RIPTA
W ripta.com

City Buses
City bus networks are generally frequent and reliable. In most cities, a single fare applies for all bus travel within city limits. Multiple trip tickets and one-day travel passes are available in major cities. Single-trip tickets can be bought from the driver when boarding, but you must pay the exact fare.

In Boston, the MBTA bus system covers much of the city, but buses are often crowded and schedules vary. Two sightseeing routes are Haymarket–Charlestown (from near Quincy Market to Bunker Hill) and Harvard–Nubian (from Harvard Square to Back Bay and South End to Nubian Square in Roxbury). The rural bus network is less extensive.

Subway
Boston's combined subway and trolley network, known as the "T", is run by the MBTA. It operates 5am–12:45am daily (from 6am on Sundays). Weekday service is every 3–15 minutes, less frequent at weekends. There are five lines: Red, from south of the city to Cambridge; Green, from the Museum of Science westward into the suburbs; Blue, from near Government Center to Logan International Airport and on to Revere; Orange, linking the northern suburbs to southwest Boston; and Silver, a surface bus that runs from Roxbury to Logan International Airport via South Station.

Admission to subway stations is via turnstiles, into which you insert a paper "Charlie" ticket or tap a plastic "Charlie" card. The plastic cards offer a discount and are intended largely for residents; visit the MBTA website for details. The paper "Charlie" ticket can be purchased at any MBTA vending machine. It can be loaded with a single trip ($2.40 subway/$1.70 bus), or a 24-hour pass ($11) or 7-day pass ($22.50), and is valid on all subway and bus routes.

Taxis

Due to the popularity of Lyft and Uber ride-hailing services, taxicabs are becoming increasingly scarce, though cabs can be still be picked up at taxi ranks and hotels in larger city centers as well as at airports. Reliable city companies include **Arrow Cab Company**, **Boston Cab**, **Cambridge Cabs**, **Green Mountain Taxi**, **Metro-Cab**, and **Royal Taxi**.

Arrow Cab Company (Hartford, CT)
W arrowcabct.com
Boston Cab (Boston, MA)
W bostoncab.us
Cambridge Cabs (Cambridge, MA)
W cambridgecabs.info
**Green Mountain Taxi
(Burlington, VA)**
W taxiinburlington.com
MetroCab (Boston, MA)
W metro-cab.com
Royal Taxi (Providence, RI)
W royaltaxiprovidence.com

Driving

Much of New England's charm is found on the region's scenic roads and on driving tours during fall-foliage season. Major cities' public transportation systems make it easy to be without a car, but driving is by far the simpliest way to explore beyond urban centers.

Driving to New England

The I-95 superhighway is the main entry to New England from New York, and runs close to the coast through Connecticut, Providence, and Rhode Island to the outskirts of Boston. Circumventing the city, the highway continues up through New Hampshire and Maine. From the north, the two major gateways into New England are I-89 and I-91. The I-89 starts in northwestern Vermont, then cuts diagonally from Burlington to Concord, New Hampshire, where it links up with I-93 into Boston. The I-91 crosses from Canada into Vermont, then follows a relatively straight line south along the Vermont/New Hampshire border, through Massachusetts and Connecticut to New Haven. The major western points of entry are I-84 and I-90 (toll road) from New York state.

Driving in New England

Driving in Boston, where traffic can be heavy and erratic and parking costly, is not advised. Most New England roads are good, with divided highways connecting most major cities. Winter and early spring driving have their challenges: snow and ice call for special driving skills, and frost heaves create sidewalk cracks and potholes. Heavy traffic can slow progress on popular roads during peak summer season.

Car Rental

To rent a car in New England you must be at least 21 years old and have a valid credit card. Some rental companies charge an extra fee to drivers under age 25. Major international car-rental agencies have outlets at all main airports and in all large towns and cities.

Rules of the Road

Third-party insurance is required. Drive on the righthand side of the road, and ensure seat belts are worn at all times by the driver and any passengers. Right turns on red (unless otherwise indicated) are allowed after coming to a complete stop. All vehicles must give way to emergency service vehicles, and traffic in both directions must stop for a school bus when signals are flashing. Pull over to call or text.

Speeding will usually result in a fine that should be paid in person if possible – the rental company will otherwise charge hefty additional admin fees. Driving under the influence (DUI) of alcohol is a very serious offence, likely leading to arrest.

Cycling

New England offers many options for cyclists of all ages and abilities. Trails in state parks, national parks, and forests are perfect off-road riding territory, and most ski resorts permit mountain biking (for a fee) in the summer. The commercial website **Bike New England** has compiled guides and links to bike routes across all of New England's six states.

Bike New England
🅦 bikenewengland.com

Bicycle Hire

Most major cities in New England have urban bike-sharing programs, some of which include electrically assisted e-bikes. Boston has **Blue Bikes** and Portland has **Portland Bikeshare**. In all cities and towns, cyclists are expected to stay off pedestrian sidewalks and follow traffic signals.

In non-urban areas, outfitters who rent canoes and kayaks usually also rent touring and mountain bikes, and can advise on local cycling routes to suit all abilities.

Blue Bikes (Boston, MA)
🅦 bluebikes.com
Portland Bikeshare (Portland, ME)
🅦 tandem-mobility.com/portland

Bike Touring

Several companies operate guided and self-guided bike tours around New England. **VBT** covers much of the region, while **Backroads** and **DuVine** focus on Vermont. **Summerfeet Cycling** specializes in Maine tours. The **Rails-to-Trails Conservancy** provides information and maps on 2,000 trails along abandoned railroad tracks that have been converted into convenient and accessible paths for cyclists and pedestrians.

Backroads
🅦 backroads.com
DuVine
🅦 duvine.com
Rails-to-Trails Conservancy
🅦 railstotrails.org
Summerfeet Cycling
🅦 summerfeet.net
VBT
🅦 vbt.com

Cycle Safety

Helmets and high-visibility clothing may not be obligatory in New England, but wearing them is strongly advised, especially when cycling in cities and on rural roads.

Walking and Hiking

Most New England city centers can be explored on foot. Even Boston is a great walking city: it is compact, and most streets are flanked by adequate sidewalks. Several different walking tours are available in Boston, most departing from the Information Center located on Boston Common. There are also many free walking tours offered by the rangers of the **Boston National Historical Park**, including segments of the Freedom Trail to Charlestown Navy Yard.

Hiking trails criss-cross almost all of New England, with the two most popular being Vermont's 265-mile (426-km) **Long Trail** and the **Appalachian Trail**. The latter stretches from Maine to Georgia and covers around 2,200 miles (3,500 km) in total, but can be broken down into shorter segments for day or multi-day hikes. If going off the beaten path, be sure you have good hiking boots, water-proof outerwear, warm inner clothing, a map, and plenty of water. Make sure your phone is fully charged, but don't count on having cell service in remote areas.

There are a number of companies that can arrange two- to five-day hiking excursions in the beautiful New England countryside. One of the best and most established operators is **Vermont Inn-to-Inn Walking**.

Appalachian Trail
🅦 appalachiantrail.org
Boston National Historical Park
🅦 nps.gov/bost
Long Trail
🅦 greenmountainclub.org/the-long-trail
Vermont Inn-to-Inn Walking
🅦 vermontinntoinnwalking.com

PRACTICAL INFORMATION

A little local know-how goes a long way in New England. On these pages you can find all the essential advice and information you will need to make the most of your trip to this region.

AT A GLANCE

CURRENCY
US Dollar (USD)

AVERAGE DAILY SPEND

SAVE	SPEND	SPLURGE
$120	$200	$300

BOTTLED WATER	COFFEE	BEER	DINNER FOR TWO
$2	$3	$8	$140

CLIMATE

The longest days occur May-Sep while Nov-Feb sees the shortest daylight hours.

Temperatures average 73°F (23°C) in summer, and regularly drop below 25°F (-4°C) in winter.

Mar-Apr and Oct-Dec see the heaviest rainfall. Expect snowfall Dec-Feb.

ELECTRICITY SUPPLY
The standard US electric current is 110 volts and 60 Hz. Power sockets are type A and B fitting plugs with two flat pins.

Passports and Visas

For entry requirements and visas, consult your nearest US embassy or the **US Department of State** before you travel, as policy changes can come into effect at short notice. All visitors to the US need a passport that is valid for six months longer than their intended period of stay. Canadian visitors only require a valid passport, but may need to register with the US government for stays of 30 days or longer. Citizens of the UK, Australia, New Zealand, and the EU do not need a visa, but must apply in advance for the Electronic System for Travel Authorization (**ESTA**); all other visitors require a visa. Visitors whose gender on their passport or visa application differs from their sex assigned at birth may face varying entry requirements and scrutiny depending on the latest US policies.

ESTA
Ⓦ esta.cbp.dhs.gov/esta
US Department of State
Ⓦ travel.state.gov

Government Advice

Now more than ever, it is important to consult both your and the US government's advice before traveling. The US Department of State, the **UK Foreign, Commonwealth and Development Office**, and the **Australian Department of Foreign Affairs and Trade** offer the latest information on security, health, and local regulations.

Australian Department of Foreign Affairs and Trade
Ⓦ smartraveller.gov.au
UK Foreign, Commonwealth and Development Office
Ⓦ gov.uk/foreign-travel-advice/usa

Customs Information

You can find information on the laws relating to goods and currency taken in or out of the US on the **Customs and Border Protection Agency** website. All

travelers need to complete a Customs and Border Protection Agency form when crossing the US border.
Customs and Border Protection Agency
w cbp.gov/travel

Insurance
We recommend that you take out a comprehensive insurance policy covering theft, loss of belongings, medical care, cancellations, and delays, and read the small print carefully. All medical treatment is private, and US health insurers do not have reciprocal arrangements with other countries. Car-rental agencies offer vehicle and liability insurance; check your policy before traveling.

Vaccinations
No inoculations are required to visit New England.

Money
Most establishments prefer major credit, debit, and prepaid currency cards. Contactless payments are now widely accepted, but it is always worth carrying some cash for smaller items and tips. Cash machines can be found at banks, airline terminals, train and bus stations, and on main streets in major towns.

Waiters will expect to be tipped 15 to 20 per cent of the total bill, hotel porters and housekeeping should be given $1 per bag or day. Round up taxi fares to at least the nearest dollar.

Travelers with Specific Requirements
All facilities renovated or newly built since 1987 are legally required to provide wheelchair-accessible entrances and restrooms. Most government buildings, museums, and theaters in New England are accessible, but call ahead to verify that tours meet your needs. It is also best to call historic buildings, hotels, and restaurants in advance to ask about amenities. Many

outdoor recreation areas have wheelchair-friendly tour buses.

Most MBTA commuter rail lines, buses, subways, and ferries accommodate wheelchairs and have audio announcements; check the MBTA website *(p140)* for details. Logan International Airport *(p140)* has accessible ramps, elevators, and restrooms, plus a list of accessible transportation to and from the airport on its website.

The **Society for Accessible Travel and Hospitality** and **Mobility International** offer information for people with specific requirements.
Mobility International
w miusa.org
Society for Accessible Travel and Hospitality
w sath.org

Language
English is the principal language spoken in New England, although Spanish is widely spoken. Some areas near the Canadian border also speak French.

Opening Hours
Most attractions and stores open daily, but many museums close on one or more days, typically early in the week. Museums are typically open from 10am to 6pm on weekdays, from 10am to 5pm on Saturday, and from noon to 5pm on Sunday. Hours and days of opening may be reduced in winter, so it is best to check beforehand with the venues. Shops typically open from 9 or 10am, and close at 6pm in business districts and at 9 or 10pm in shopping centers (they close at 6pm on weekends).

Some banks open on Saturday mornings, but outside of the bigger cities, many stay closed on weekends.

Situations can change quickly and unexpectedly. Always check before visiting attractions and hospitality venues for up-to-date opening hours and booking requirements.

Personal Security

New England is generally safe, but petty crime does take place. Pickpockets work known tourist areas and busy streets. Use your common sense, keep valuables in a safe place, and be alert to your surroundings. If you have anything stolen, report the crime as soon as possible at the nearest police station. Get a copy of the crime report to claim on your insurance. Contact your embassy or consulate immediately if your passport is stolen or in the event of a serious crime or accident.

As a rule, New Englanders are very accepting of all people, regardless of their race, gender, or sexuality. The country's abolitionist and women's suffrage movements both started here, and the region was early to support same-sex marriage. In fact, Vermont was the first US state to introduce civil unions in 2000, and Massachusetts became the first state to legalize same-sex marriage in 2004. Today, Boston has the largest LGBTQ+ population in the region, but even small towns are accepting. If you do feel unsafe, the **Safe Space Alliance** pinpoints your nearest place of refuge.

Safe Space Alliance

w safespacealliance.com

Health

New England has a world-class health system, with a number of acclaimed hospitals. However, as the US does not have a government health program, emergency medical and dental care can be very expensive. Medical travel insurance is highly recommended in order to cover some of the costs. If you are able, call the number on your insurance policy first, and check which hospitals your insurance company deals with.

If you need a prescription dispensed, there are pharmacies (drugstores) in every city in the region, some staying open 24 hours. Ask your hotel for the nearest one.

Smoking, Alcohol, and Drugs

Smoking and vaping are banned in all public spaces such as bus and train stations, airports, and enclosed areas of bars, cafés, restaurants, and hotels. However, some bars and restaurants have designated outdoor areas where smoking is permitted.

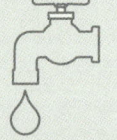

Alcohol may not be sold to or bought for anyone under the age of 21 in the US. The drink-drive limit is strictly enforced, so it's best to avoid drinking alcohol if you plan to drive.

Recreational cannabis use is decriminalized in New Hampshire and fully legal in all other New England states; however, public consumption is largely discouraged. There is no objective standard of impairment if a driver has been using cannabis, but operating a vehicle while under the influence is a crime.

ID
Passports are required as ID at airports. (American citizens may use a state driver's license to board domestic flights.) Anyone who looks under 25 may be asked for photo ID to prove their age when buying alcohol or tobacco.

Responsible Tourism
Long considered one of the US's most environmentally conscious regions, New England continues to gain national acclaim for its forward-thinking initiatives and policies. Boston is recognized by the Natural Resources Defense Council as the greenest city on the East Coast; and both Maine and Vermont are national leaders in environmental initiatives. Recycling facilities are common, and community farmers' markets selling local produce and artisan foodstuffs can be found in every corner of every state. Visitors can also help towards the region's sustainable goals by cycling or walking around city centers, and using reusable bags and water bottles when out and about.

Cell Phones and Wi-Fi
Do not rely on cell phones or other devices for navigation or emergency communications in remote areas such as northern Maine and New Hampshire, where signal can be intermittent.

Free Wi-Fi is also usually found at public libraries and coffee shops, as well as many public parks and hotels.

Visitors from outside the US can buy pay-as-you-go SIM cards at airports and most phone stores, which can be used in compatible phones. Canadian residents can usually upgrade their domestic cell-phone plan to extend to the US. Pre-paid phone cards usually offer the best rates for long-distance calls, and are sold in most drugstores.

Post
The majority of post offices are open from 8am to 6pm Monday to Friday and 8am to noon Saturday. Properly stamped letters and packages less than 12 oz (340 g) can be dropped into blue mailboxes. For current rates, see the **US Postal Service** website.
US Postal Service
w usps.com

Taxes and Refunds
It is important to remember that listed prices rarely include applicable taxes. All New England states, with the exception of New Hampshire, levy their own sales tax (usually somewhere between 5 and 8 per cent). All states charge taxes on hotel rooms and restaurant meals, and some cities also have tax surcharges. Since none of these taxes is levied at a national level, international visitors cannot claim refunds.

Visitor Information
Many New England museums, galleries, and attractions offer discounts to students and senior citizens. A valid form of ID is required. Students from abroad should carry an International Student Identity Card (**ISIC**) to claim discounts on hostel accommodation, museums, and theaters. Over-50s should look into buying an **AARP** membership (open to non-Americans), which can provide discounts at hotels and on car rentals.
AARP
w aarp.org
ISIC
w isic.org

PLACES TO STAY

Whether you want to hunker down in a bed and breakfast in the mountains, unwind in a luxury boutique by the sea, or explore the capital from a historic hotel in Boston, New England has accommodation to suit every taste.

Lodgings can fill up and prices shoot up during key seasons, particularly when it comes to coastal hotels in the summer and ski resorts in the winter. The greatest concentration of properties can be found in Boston, an ideal base for exploring the region.

PRICE CATEGORIES

For a standard, double room per night (with breakfast if included), taxes and extra charges.

$ under $300
$$ $300–$500
$$$ over $500

Massachusetts

Boston Harbor Hotel
📍X4 🏠70 Rowes Wharf, Boston 🌐 bostonharbor hotel.com · $$$

Overlooking the water and featuring a huge arched entryway, this five-star hotel is an icon on the city's waterfront. It's equally impressive inside. Suites promise marble bathrooms and gorgeous waterside views, the wellness center features state-of-the-art fitness spaces, and the on-site restaurant is a seafood-lover's dream. This is a world-class hotel, befitting a world-class city.

The Liberty
📍V3 🏠215 Charles St, Boston 🌐 libertyhotel.com · $$$

Few successful vacations involve a stay in jail, unless you're checking in here. A prison from 1851 to 1990, this space has been elegantly revamped, but still wears its history on its sleeve; seasonal fare is served at the restaurant, CLINK, celebrity mugshots line the walls of the bar, Alibi, and the mezzanine has features of the original cells. This is a place you'll willingly do time in.

YOTEL Boston
📍X4 🏠62 Seaport Blvd, Boston 🌐 yotel.com · $

Cool and lively, this affordable spot is a favorite among young travelers. The highlight is the buzzy rooftop bar, Deck 12, which offers live music, weekend brunch, and housemade frosé (a refreshing blend of ice, fruit, and rosé) on Fridays. Cheers to that.

The Lenox Hotel
📍U4 🏠61 Exeter St, Boston 🌐 lenoxhotel.com · $$

The Lenox has some serious eco cred. Hallways feature filtered-water stations, bathrooms are stocked with locally sourced toiletries, and the restaurant and bar use honey harvested from the rooftop beehives. It's a lovely place to retreat to after seeing Boston by bike (which you can rent from the hotel, by the way).

The Verb Hotel
📍S5 🏠1271 Boylston St, Boston 🌐 theverbhotel. com · $$

Music lovers, this one's for you. Steps away from Fenway Park, the Verb is a love letter to rock 'n' roll, with vinyl records, band posters, and guitars lining the walls. Each room comes with a turntable, too – there's an extensive selection of albums available in the lobby, which you can borrow.

Ocean Edge Resort and Golf Club
📍H4 🏠2907 Main St, Brewster 🌐 oceanedge. com · $$

Live it up in this lavish Cape Cod estate with a private beach and host of great restaurants. Rooms range from mansion accommodations to family-friendly villas, complete with kitchenettes. There's also a golf course, tennis courts, five swimming pools, and a beach bar.

Greydon House

📍 H5 🏠 117 Broad St, Nantucket 🌐 greydonhouse.com · $$$

In the heart of Nantucket's historic downtown and a short stroll from the ferry terminal, this elegant boutique couldn't be better placed. But it's not just the location that keeps guests coming back. This former sea captain's house is beautifully finished, with touches of both the historical and the modern (think nautical antiques, handpainted tiles, and locally inspired artwork). It's Nantucket at its best.

The Christopher

📍 G5 🏠 24 S Water St, Edgartown 🌐 theedgartowncollection.com · $$$

It's hard to pick a stand-out feature at the Christopher. This Martha's Vineyard boutique is beloved for its ever-friendly staff, chic decor, and great location (in central Edgartown). But then there's the breakfast (which is always tasty), the beds (promising luxurious sheets), and the atmospheric courtyard (complete with a fire pit). Essentially, it's all great.

Devonfield Inn

📍 B3 🏠 85 Stockbridge Rd, Lee 🌐 devonfield.com · $$$

Want to retreat to the countryside, but don't want to leave behind the luxury? Look no further than this gorgeous, 1800-era inn. Set within acres of land in the Berkshires, and close to hiking trails, leaf-peeping spots, and ski runs, the Devonfield is perfect for outdoorsy travelers. After enjoying a day in the countryside, guests can return to a wood-burning fire, songs around the baby grand piano, and complimentary cognac in the living room. This place is hard to resist.

Rhode Island

The Break Hotel

📍 E5 🏠 1208 Ocean Rd, Narragansett 🌐 thebreahhotel.com · $$

It's easy to unwind at this breezy, beachside hotel. A go-to on Rhode Island's coast, the Break Hotel is located just a short walk (or cycle – bikes are free to rent) from the water, and many of its rooms have sweeping sea views, too. Other perks include an outdoor pool (heated, unlike the sea here) and a sunny rooftop bar (which serves seafood under the sunset).

The Beatrice

📍 E4 🏠 90 Westminster St, Providence 🌐 thebeatrice.com · $$

Check in to the Beatrice and you might not want to leave. This downtown Providence gem brings modern elegance to the city, with thoughtful design touches like heated bidet toilets, cozy bathrobes, luxury personal-care amenities, and bathroom speakers. You don't need to leave the hotel for food, either: the Beatrice hosts a scenic rooftop bar and a top-notch restaurant, too.

Forty 1° North

📍 F5 🏠 351 Thames St, Newport 🌐 41north.com · $$$

Luxury meets sustainability at Forty 1° North, Rhode Island's first LEED-certified hotel. The sustainability credentials are great, but you'll be more than a little distracted by the luxury. Wow-worthy rooms are spacious and elegant, the hotel's numerous bars and restaurants are destinations in themselves, and then there are the views. Set on the marina, the hotel promises stunning sunsets and glimpses of the luxurious yachts that dock here.

Blue Whale Inn

📍 E5 🏠 54 Winnapaug Rd, Misquamicut 🌐 staybluewhale.com · $

It's not always easy to find a good deal in New England, but the Blue Whale Inn is just that. This affordable Rhode Island inn features charming (if small) rooms, a tranquil garden, and beach access. Complimentary beach chairs, umbrellas, and wagons are up for grabs to make your beach day easier, too.

Connecticut

The Goodwin Hotel

C4 **1** Haynes St, Hartford **W** goodwin hartford.com · $$

The perfect base in Hartford, this landmark hotel was originally an apartment block, built in the Queen Anne architectural style in 1881. Now converted into a hotel, it seemlessly fuses historical features with modern additions: many rooms showcase original fireplaces and restored built-in wood closets, while the hotel also offers a fitness center, and all rooms have flat-screen TVs.

Hotel Marcel

C5 **500** Sargent Dr, New Haven **W** hotel marcel.com · $

Bauhaus meets Brutalism at this striking hotel. A mammoth concrete building designed in the 1960s, this architectural icon is now one of the greenest hotels in the country, running entirely on renewable energy. Minimalist rooms feature state-of-the-art tech and sleek, Bauhaus-inspired furnishings. It's close to Yale University, too.

The Griswold Inn

D5 **36** Main St, Essex **W** griswoldinn.com · $$

Step back in time at the Griswold Inn. This 1776-era venue is one of the oldest continuously run inns in the US – spot the original beamed ceilings and wealth of maritime-themed art from over the years. Be sure to check out the inn's popular taproom – it hosts sea-shanty performances.

Winvian

B4 **155** Alain White Rd, Morris **W** winvian.com · $$$

Stay in a converted helicopter, a suspended treehouse, or a quirky log cabin: the Winvian has it all. This luxury estate is located in the scenic Litchfield Hills and comprises 18 uniquely designed cottages, plus an acclaimed restaurant. If the whimsical cottages aren't enough, there are numerous activities on offer, too – tarot reading, cooking classes, and sound therapy, to name a few.

Vermont

Green Mountain Inn

K3 **18** Main St, Stowe, **W** greenmountaininn. com · $

The Green Mountain Inn has been an affordable base in Vermont since way back in 1833. Its 101 accommodations span suites and townhouses, while contemporary amenities include a pool, hot tub, and fitness center.

Hill Farm

J6 **458** Hill Farm Rd, Sunderland **W** hillfarminn.com · $$

Part of a working farm, this quaint hotel makes for a quintessential rural Vermont escape. Guests can spot alpacas in the fields, walk along the property's river path, or feast on locally sourced food in the restaurant.

Woodstock Inn and Resort

K5 **14** The Green, Woodstock **W** woodstock inn.com · $$

Cozy up at this classic Vermont resort, close to the charming village of Woodstock. It's arguably at its best during winter, when folks go skiing and snowshoeing during the mornings and return for afternoons spent unwinding at the gorgeous spa and pool or warming up by the lobby fireplace.

Twin Farms

K4 **452** Royalton Turnpike **W** twinfarms. com · $$$

Live out your fall fantasy in this 18th-century farmhouse estate, set within 300 acres of leafy countryside. Each of its 28 cottages and suites are unique, while gourmet dining, bespoke outdoor adventures, and luxurious spa appointments are all available. It's a secluded, all-inclusive experience, and the leaf-peeping is great, too.

Swift House Inn

J4 **57** N Pleasant St, Middlebury **W** swift houseinn.com · $

This 1800s-era estate has mastered the art of rustic New England hospitality with well-appointed rooms, attentive staff, and, best of all, a spectacular restaurant. Dining here is a highlight thanks to the delicious homemade breakfasts and modern American fare for dinner.

New Hampshire

Omni Mount Washington Resort and Spa

M3 **310 Mount Washington Hotel Rd, Bretton Woods** W omni hotels.com · **$$$**

You'll never be short on things to do at this vast resort in New Hampshire's moutains. Tee off on the 18-hole golf course, go horse riding through the countryside, fly above the trees on a thrilling zipline, go snow tubing on the nearby slopes…the list goes on. Outdoor adventure is front-and-center here, but there are more relaxing amenities, too: the spa has a variety of pools, and there's a plethora of restaurants to choose from.

Chesterfield Inn

K6 **20 Cross Rd, West Chesterfield** W chester fieldinn.com · **$**

Surrounded by wild-flower meadows and shady trees, this lovely, countryside inn promises a truly romantic escape. Rooms are spacious and beautifully appointed – some have private balconies or deck areas, while others feature cozy fireplaces. The gourmet breakfast is a real treat.

The Hotel Concord

M5 **11 S Main St, Concord** W hotelconcord nh.com · **$**

The capital's favorite boutique, the Hotel Concord is sleek, modern, and ideally located in the downtown area. In addition to promising classic amenities, it also offers a 24-hour gym and access to an on-site movie theater.

Grand View Resort

M5 **291 Endicott St N, Laconia** W grandviewnh. com · **$**

Planning a kid-friendly getaway? Look no further than this resort near Lake Winnipesaukee. The renovated cabins are perfect for families, with lake access, a large, saltwater pool, and an ice-cream parlor next door. Summer sorted.

Maine

Bluenose Inn

R3 **90 Eden St, Bar Harbor** W barharborhotel. com/bluenose-inn · **$$**

Scenically located on Mount Desert Island, this stately hotel is the perfect base for exploring Acadia National Park – numerous hikes can be found in the local area. The hotel itself features both indoor and outdoor pools and spacious rooms with private balconies. But the Bluenose Inn has one more ace up its sleeve: head down to the piano lounge and you'll be greeted by live music nearly every night.

Cliff House Maine

N5 **591 Shore Rd, Cape Neddick** W cliff housemaine.com · **$$$**

Ocean views don't get much better than this. Sprawled across a cliff-side battered by waves, this dreamy resort has been drawing vacationers since 1872. And not just for its sea views. Atlantic-facing suites promise private balconies, the gym offers group classes, and the dining options are top-tier.

Wolf Cove Inn

N4 **5 Jordan Shore Dr, Poland** W wolfcoveinn. com · **$$**

Spend your days by the water at this enchanting inn. Wolf Cove Inn sits right on the shores of Tripp Lake, and it makes the most of its scenic location. Most rooms have picture-perfect lake views, but if you don't get lucky, just head outside: complimentary kayaks make outdoor adventuring a breeze, while the lakeside fire pit is perfect for relaxing.

The Press Hotel, Autograph Collection

N4 **119 Exchange St, Portland** W thepresshotel. com · **$$**

Once home to the *Portland Press Herald*, this boutique property pays homage to its roots with typewriter art and old-school journalist desks. It's close to Portland's main attractions, too.

INDEX

ACKNOWLEDGMENTS

This edition updated by

Contributor Jared Ranahan

Senior Editor Keith Drew

Senior Designer Vinita Venugopal

Project Editor Lucy Sara-Kelly

Project Art Editor Nidhi Mehra

Editor Pankhoori Sinha

Proofreader Ruth Reisenberger

Indexer Helen Peters

Deputy Picture Research Manager Virien Chopra

Senior Picture Researcher Nishwan Rasool

Assistant Picture Research Administrator Manpreet Kaur

Publishing Assistants Serena Sclocco, Simona Velikova

Jacket Designers Katie Cavanagh, Nidhi Mehra

Jacket Picture Researcher Laura O'Brien

Project Cartographer Ashif

Cartography Manager Suresh Kumar

Pre-Production Coordinator Tanveer Zaidi

Pre-Production Designer Rohit Rojal

Pre-Production Image Editor Nityanand Kumar

Pre-Production Manager Balwant Singh

Pre-Production Image Manager Pankaj Sharma

Production Controller Kariss Ainsworth

Deputy Managing Editor Dharini Ganesh

Managing Editor Beverly Smart

Managing Art Editor Gemma Doyle

Senior Managing Art Editor Priyanka Thakur

Editorial Director Hollie Teague

Art Director Maxine Pedliham

Publishing Director Georgina Dee

DK would like to thank the following for their contribution to the previous editions: Kathryn Glendenning, Patricia Harris, and David Lyon.

The publisher would like to thank the following for their kind permission to reproduce their photographs:

Key: a-above; b-below/bottom; c-center; f-far; l-left; r-right; t-top

First edition 2010

Published in Great Britain by Dorling
Kindersley Limited, DK, 20 Vauxhall Bridge Road,
London SW1V 2SA.

The authorised representative in the EEA is
Dorling Kindersley Verlag GmbH. Arnulfstr.
124, 80636 Munich, Germany.

Published in the United States by DK Publishing,
1745 Broadway, 20th Floor, New York, NY 10019, USA.

The publishers cannot accept responsibility for any consequences
arising from the use of this book, nor for any material on third
party websites, and cannot guarantee that any website address
in this book will be a suitable source of travel information.

A CIP catalog record for this book
is available from the British Library.

A catalog record for this book is available
from the Library of Congress.

ISSN: 1479-344X
ISBN: 978 0 2417 8364 1

Printed and bound in China

www.dk.com

This book was made with Forest
Stewardship Council™ certified
paper – one small step in DK's
commitment to a sustainable future.
Learn more at **www.dk.com/uk/
information/sustainability**